When
The Road
Bends

A Book about the Pain and Joy of Passage

When The Road Bends

Karl A. Olsson

AUGSBURG Publishing House • Minneapolis

When The Road Bends

Preface

Many years ago I became interested in the universal social phenomena identified by Arnold van Gennep, a 19th-century French anthropologist, as *rites de passage* and *rites de saison* (rites of passage and rites of season). Three years ago, when the formal academic scene lay far behind me, I found practical meaning in these categories, and I began to ask how the Christian faith ministers to people undergoing the pains of passage. I started working on a manuscript dealing with these pains, and I wrote an article for the January 1975 issue of *Faith at Work* magazine called "Pain of Passage."

In late summer of that year I began to rethink my manuscript in terms of the triad of passage, ritual, and process, and I tested out the validity of a procedure that not only recognizes passages but moves on to ritualize passage, as well as interpreting and assimilating it. While at work on this task, I began to discover how significant passage, ritual, and process were to our Lord and to the primitive church. I went back to my manuscript in an effort to put all this together, and I found the orchestration almost beyond my powers.

Personal acknowledgments may not belong in prefaces, but I would like to break precedent by saying how much the periodic resuscitation of this book has been due to the faith and practical suggestions of my wife Sally and my friends and coworkers at Augsburg Publishing House. Several times when I was ready to abandon the project, their encouragement motivated me to return to it, and I am grateful. I also owe special thanks to Marie Moore and Sarah McCarthy, who helped me by typing the manuscript in its several versions and by being unfailingly present to me in the process.

In this book I have tried to include, along with facts about the human experience of passage, some theological insights about this experience and some suggestions about how such an experience can be processed within the sharing and caring community of the church. I hope it will serve as both an idea book and a how-to book for those struggling like me with the pain and the glory of our pilgrimage through time.

The everlasting now

In times of rapid change, the claims of stable institutions and those of risking individuals and groups become polarized. The situation is not unlike the conflict between insecure parents and their adolescent children. The institution builds its defenses of tradition and precedent and dares the innovators to attack. The innovators, frustrated by the power and stubbornness of the institution and frenzied by the desire for more freedom, hammer with bloodied fists at the defenses of the establishment and the *status quo*. Gradually, as the frustration level rises, innovators become iconoclasts, praying for the rapid destruction of the entire institutional defense system. And threatened by radical attacks, the guardians of "what is and has been" dig in even more desperately and stake their lives on winning the siege.

In this process of action and reaction, thesis and antithesis, the coloring of the situation changes in the minds of the opponents from shades of gray to black and white. Opponents are now enemies and even demons, and the struggle becomes a holy war.

A few years ago, when relational theology, process, and life-style became live options for growing numbers of people in the established churches, polarization began. The institutional church was accused of being pompous and static; those interested in group process and a freer life-style were looked on with suspicion. Some took an either-or stance. Either you were a friend of the established churches or you were their enemy. Either you made relational theology your only frame of reference or you were discredited as a fossil and a Pharisee.

I confess that there was a time when, in my enthusiasm for the relational life-style, I felt less than sympathetic with what seemed to me the insensitivity and procedural conservatism of leaders in the established churches. I remain as deeply committed as ever to a life-style that, through the power of the Holy Spirit and the agency of some wonderfully open and accepting people, became a life-changing discovery for me. But I am developing greater awareness of the totality of time and existence and of the need to integrate both past and future into the present.

Matthew Arnold once thanked Sophocles because the great Greek tragedian "saw life steadily and saw it whole." Because I am theoretically and practically committed to wholeness, I am praying for a wisdom that sees time as a continuous line and hence gives all history its due. C.H. Dodd once helped me to see that in the Scriptures, theology is almost unvaryingly stated as history. The substance of biblical theology lies in God's mighty acts on our behalf and our actions as a response to those acts. Divine acts cover all of created time: past, present, and future. Christ, the Logos, is the culmination of God's activity on our behalf.

This means that, as a believing Christian, I cannot ignore history, either my own personal history or the history of the race, or, more specifically, the history of the people of God. If I break the continuity of that history, I strip myself of some of my being and some of my destiny.

I want to continue to "live in the now," "celebrate the temporary," and "kiss the joy," but I want to claim the *now* without losing touch with the *then*.

I see God's presence in all of history when I look at the historic churches, their traditions and rituals, their rites of passage and season. In them I see mirrored the struggles of people long-since dead, how they strove to meet the crises of their passages through time. In the rituals and traditions I see how people related their faith in the God of history to the flux of pain and joy, hope and despair.

In the presence of the mountainous massifs of past time—the vast volcanic peaks of history—and in the presence of the volcanic boilings, spoutings, and flowings of the present, St. Augustine's words in the *Confessions* become luminous for me:

> For thou art most high, and art not changed, neither in thee doth today come to a close; yet in thee doth it come to a close; because all such things also are in thee. For they had no way to pass away, unless thou upheldest them. And since thy years fail not, thy years are one today. How many of ours and our fathers' years have flowed away through thy today, and from it received the measure and the mould of such being as they had; and still others shall flow away, and so receive the mould of their degree of being. But thou art still the same, all things of tomorrow, and all beyond, and all of yesterday, and all behind it, thou hast done today.

Because it is a ritual framework, the church, regardless of its beliefs and mode of worship, tends to *repeat,* that is, to celebrate "our fathers' years." It works with recurrence rather than occurrence. This is valid as one of its functions, but we cannot be content with merely repeating rites. There is a greater solidarity than the solidarity of memory. We worship the God of history, who in Christ creates, inhabits, and transcends time. In remembering the past and being mindful of traditions and rituals, we claim the presence of Christ as the risen and

11

living Lord. We claim his presence in his own history, in his experience of the pains and joys of human passage. We claim his presence in our current history within his body, when, because of his nearness, we are able to process our passages with acceptance and hope. And we claim his presence at the end of history, when passages are no more and ritual is gathered up in the ultimate song of adoration, "to him who sits on the throne and to the Lamb."

Because of him, all of our yesterdays and all of our tomorrows are "one today." They are parts of that which, in Augustine's words, "thou hast done today." Because of God, our entire existence is an everlasting now. That is what I try to say in this book.

PART I

"OURS AND OUR FATHERS' YEARS"

ONE

TIME AND DEATH

In the midst of a pain that both harasses and puzzles him, Job summarizes the human lot in an axiom: "Man that is born of a woman is of few days, and full of trouble [anxiety]. He comes forth like a flower, and withers; he flees like a shadow, and continues not" (Job 14:1-2).

Because human beings are reflective (Pascal calls us thinking reeds), the brevity of our time on earth is a source of anxiety. Every moment carries its freight of death. Death is not just a chance episode, the result of an accident or an illness that cuts life short; it is integral to life, at least as we know it.

There is hence no little pathos in our society's preoccupation with the prevention of what we might call "episodic death." To avoid such death, we ask for safety in soda pop, cranberries, jelly beans, cigarettes. We seek to circumvent it by seat belts, self-inflating impact bags, jogging, frequent visits to the doctor, granola, and watching our weight.

Such concerns are, of course, legitimate, for we have an obligation to make life as safe as possible.

But the obsession with episodic death may keep us from facing a grimmer reality, namely, that no matter how secure our life becomes in terms of germs, carcinogenic agents, world peace, ecology, or a just distribution of goods, we are still going to die.

Some years ago our four-year-old granddaughter came into the bathroom to watch me shaving. Something in my graying beard and seamed face must have struck her, for she said to me, "Poor you!" "Poor me?" I asked. "Why 'poor me'?" "Because you're going to die," she said. "When you die, you go to sleep and you don't wake up." Then she was gone, and I stood staring into the mirror, both amused and terrified.

Of course, we all know this, but we try not to think about it. We are somewhat in the position of Oedipus, the king who tries to remain blind to the truth that he has unwittingly killed his father and married his mother. As the facts move in on him, he becomes increasingly defensive and irascible. We witness the spectacle of a man who clings more and more desperately to the rock of denial, until reality washes over him and he drowns.

Like that ancient king, most of us use every stratagem available to us to blind ourselves to the truth that, in Job's words, "we come forth like a flower and wither."

Perhaps it is our general evasiveness of the subject of death that makes the comedy of Woody Allen speak to us so powerfully. Allen often casts himself as a character who, in contrast to "beautiful people" with their sophisticated dress and suave manners, hasn't got his stuff together. He is a hypochondriac, with a drugstore of medications in his bathroom· cabinet. He is homely, slight, freckled, droop-faced, and he lacks the obvious signs of masculinity and *machismo*. When, despite his brittleness, he is able to attract beautiful and gifted women, he pushes them away. When his gifts bring him close to fame and its rewards, he flees in panic.

In *Annie Hall,* his Oscar-winning movie, Woody is juxtaposed with the Hollywood crowd in an unforgettable Christmas scene, every moment of which is a denial of the reality of death. Woody, gauche, awkward, and feather-light in his unimpressiveness, is set over against "beautiful people" who, by one trick or another, deny their humanity and their mortality. To them Woody is a "killjoy at the feast" who stirs up enough of their shadowy selves to make them uncomfortable, but ultimately only activates them to stauncher denial. The windmill persons against whom Woody tilts live in the illusion that they will never die, whereas he is confident that he will be carried off at any moment.

Our curious doubleness on this point—our awareness of death and our denial of it—may account for the enormous popularity of J. R. R. Tolkien's *The Lord of the Rings.* Tolkien claims that the theme of his trilogy is "the inevitability of death." He writes: "If you really come down to any really large story that interests people and hold their attention for a considerable time, it is practically always a human story and it is practically always about one thing all the time: death, the inevitability of death." [1]

17

We can agree with Tolkien that serious works of art—that is, those dealing with our darker fates— have universal appeal. In declines of fortune, the inevitability of death is sensed. But Tolkien overlooks one significant point. A work of art dealing with death may, by the very fact that it is art and not reality, help us evade the subject. After all, the person who dies in the story is not I, and it is not my death.

The most powerful fictional description of death I know is Tolstoy's *The Death of Ivan Ilych.* I once read that long short story at one sitting. I came close to understanding what the apostle Paul means when he writes about his revelations, "whether in the body or out of the body I do not know." During the reading I was totally absorbed, and when I lifted my eyes from the page, my teeth were clenched shut, my mouth was dry, my body was trembling, and my heart was beating rapidly. I felt, as I had not felt before, the existential despair that can arise from one man's imaginings of the pangs of death. But despite my almost violent kinetic response to the story, it remained for me a story, a work of art. It was not the death of Ivan Ilych, but a story about it. That experience strengthened my conviction that an artistic event, such as reading or seeing a tragedy, may serve to bring death closer, but it may also help me to push it farther away.

This may be what the Spanish thinker Ortega y Gasset means when he speaks of civilization as humanity's frantic effort to escape death. He writes:

> Existence is a continuous shipwreck. But to experience a shipwreck is not to drown. The pitiable human being, who senses that he is sinking into the abyss, begins to move his arms to stay afloat. This motion of the arms by which he reacts against his own destruction is culture or civilization. . . . Deliverance lies in the awareness that shipwreck is the truth about life. Hence human beings must be placed before the judgment seat of that living reality.[2]

Ritual: A means of coping

A primitive, if not the most primitive, art form in which we discern the "motion of the arms" is the ritual. The ritual is a solemn, repeated act symbolizing a significant experience in the life of the individual or people. The word *symbolize* is important. The ritual is not identical with the original action. It points back to the action.

For example, a puberty rite signals the onset of maturity in the lives of boys and girls but is not that onset. The isolation of the child from the tribe and the painful and joyous reintegration of that child into the tribe, which figure in many puberty rites, symbolize the shedding of childhood status and the readiness to assume the freer but also more responsible role of the adult.

The symbolic act of the ritual seems to be a way of coping with or even controlling the pain attending passage. In symbolizing the passage from child to adult, the puberty rite carries with it a constellation of feelings, many of which are positive. It celebrates the role of the community in blessing and equipping the child. It acknowledges the surge of life and fertility that puberty activates. It recognizes the health and normalcy of growth and change. But it also mourns the loss of childhood: its freedom, its playfulness, its dependency, its special charm. In thus confronting the truth of time and death, it provides a "swimming motion" by means of which the pain of passage is assuaged and in some ways transcended.

Funeral ceremonies also are symbolic enactments. The funeral is not the death; it provides a symbolic way of dealing with death. Something must be done with the dead body, both actually and symbolically, no matter how artfully it is masked. Thomas Shepard, a 17th-century American theologian, writes, "Abraham loved Sarah, but when she died, he buried her." It took me a long time to see that Shepard was doing more than stating the obvious. He was providing a biblical model for an act which, of all those surrounding death, is the most difficult, the one we resist most strongly.

Burial symbolizes the isolation and separation that death has brought. In some sense the dead person must now be put out of our life. There is no way of getting around that. Some well-intentioned funeral directors and pastors try to make it easier on the mourners by not having them present at the graveside, but interment is a powerful symbol of what has happened. Depriving the funeral service of this appearance before the judgment seat of reality reduces the power of consolation. Limiting the ritual to a stress on what death cannot take away—a person's lasting impact on the family and community, and even the hope of a life to come—is like

20

swimming with one arm. The rationale of the ritual is to feel the intensity of the pain of passage and to deal with it ceremonially. Only thus can it be cleanly integrated.

Rituals draw on history

Historic religions add a dimension to the symbolism of the ritual. They introduce a person or event out of the past as a model for the present. Thus, in the Christian tradition the passage of the people of Israel through the Red Sea prefigures God's mighty act in raising Jesus from the dead. It symbolizes the Christian believer's death and resurrection in Baptism.

We are creatures who "look before and after" (Shelley), who remember and anticipate, and we use rituals to draw the past into the present in order to cope with the future. Faced with the fragile quality of our own existence, we use the ritual to claim the power of the ancient symbol and to be nourished by the presence, support, and blessing of the believing community.

In *Freud, Goethe, and Wagner,* Thomas Mann gives moving expression to this phenomenon:

> A feast is an anniversary, a renewal of the past in the present. Every Christmas the world-saving Babe is born again on earth, to suffer, to die, and to arise. The feast is the abrogation of time, an event, a solemn narrative being played out conformably to an immemorial pattern; the events in it take place not for the first time, but ceremonially, according to the prototype. It achieves presentness as feasts do, recurring in

time with their phases and hours following on each other in time as they did in the original occurrence.

Evidence of the need for ritualization even among the Russian people, who have officially denounced their ancient religious symbols, was provided in the National Geographic documentary, *The Volga*. The film made clear that, although the Russian Orthodox Church no longer plays its historic role in the life of the people, the people are less committed to the goals of the party than to ritualizing the events of their personal and corporate existence. The film showed memorial celebrations at Volgograd in which the horror and glory of the World War II siege were remembered by masses of contemporary Russian people. These celebrations were a ritual experience with strong religious overtones. The elimination of Christian symbols except within the walls of a few carefully selected churches has not eliminated faith, theology, or religious celebration from the Soviet Union. It seems only to have raised Mother Russia to the redemptive role formerly assigned to the Blessed Virgin and has made Lenin, whose face is iconized throughout the USSR, into her firstborn son. That Lenin strenuously resisted such adoration is beside the point. The need for a hero-savior has robbed him of his humanity and, ironically, made him into the red god.

What the Russian people seem to celebrate on every ritual occasion, if we can trust the film, is the wounding, dying, and rebirth of revolutionary Russia—the blood of the past is the price for the present.

This impression was strengthened by my 1977 visit to the USSR. On VE Day, signaling the end of the European phase of World War II, the Russians give themselves a two-day holiday of remembrance. In Leningrad public buildings were splotched with gigantic banners and bunting in the bloody colors of the revolution, and the streets were jammed with holiday crowds, whose solemn deportment gave the whole city the air of a church service. The old transcendent symbols may have lost their power for the majority of the people, but the USSR has proceeded to create a new transcendence out of the mighty acts of its fallen heroes.

Even a thoroughly secularized wedding ceremony pictured in the documentary film showed the bride and bridegroom not only receiving official sanction for their marriage in a civic ceremony (which seemed unusually clumsy), but also capping their vows by placing flowers on the graves of dead Soviet soldiers. It was almost as though they expected to derive energy from the tomb to face what lay before them, not unlike the blessing sought by medieval pilgrims at the tomb of Thomas Becket and St. James of Compostela.

Such ritualization, whether ancient or modern, theistic or atheistic, must be seen as one of those desperate "swimming motions" by which we human beings try to keep life from being meaningless and unendurable.

C. S. Lewis sees ritual as this kind of essential and hence inevitable strategy. In *A Preface to Paradise Lost,* he writes:

It [ritual] is a pattern imposed on the mere flux of our feelings by reason and will which renders pleasures less fugitive and griefs more endurable, which hands over to the power of wise custom the task (to which the individual and his moods are so inadequate) of being festive or sober, gay or reverent, when we choose to be and not at the bidding of chance.

Life cycles and annual cycles

Ritual devices designed to deal with the twin problems of time and death emerge in both the life cycles and the annual cycles of most peoples. Few, if any, of those societies observed by anthropologists make nothing of birth, puberty, marriage, the birthing of children, aging, and death. Within the Judaeo-Christian tradition, prophetic religion has overlaid the rites of passage with novel and subtle meanings, but the primal outline may still be discerned in such ceremonial acts as circumcision and Baptism, Bar Mitzvah and confirmation.

The annual cycle is the basis for rites of season. In older cultures the time of sowing was closely associated with fertility rites. Seedtime and harvest were prime seasonal celebrations. Because of the connection between the sunlight and growth, the return and consummation of the light (the solstice) became a particular time for festivity. In the northern hemisphere, the Christmas season and midsummer eves celebrated these solstices.

Our modern cyclical religious holidays build on these recurring times in the annual cycles, even though these have long ago been overlaid by happenings in the history of faith. Thus the festivals of Christmas and Easter, although they celebrate historic events, are congruent with the winter solstice and the spring equinox. They signal not only relatively recent happenings, but also the relentless moving of the clock of time. The rite of season becomes a rite of passage.

This is particularly true of Christmas. Seen generally as a joyous festival celebrating the lighting of candles in the winter dark, Christmas nevertheless has a sad counterpoint. It mingles the sweetness of human love and caring with the bitterness of mortality and the passing of time. For many people the best of Christmases seems consequently tinged with grief and anxiety.

Dr. Walt Menninger cites a number of psychotherapists who have struggled with the anxiety and depression that Christmas seems to induce in some people. He writes:

> The holidays serve to remind people of the passage of time, as well as their dependence on one another. Thus, despite the joyful nature of the holidays, few people live through them without some emotional pain—anxiety, disappointment, sadness.
>
> Psychoanalyst George Pollock has called attention to the purpose of festivals celebrating the holiday and the new year. They help us reflect on past and future, and our relationships to ourselves, family, and God. Yet the passage of time is evidence of progress of life toward death. Not surprisingly the toasts and congratulations often focus on gratitude for having lived another year.
>
> This revelation of self and life can produce anxiety. . . . The most extreme (holiday) reaction has been described by another psychoana-

lyst, James Cattell. His "holiday syndrome" is characterized by diffuse anxiety, marked feelings of helplessness, increased irritability, nostalgia or bitter ruminations about holiday experiences of youth, depression, and a wish for a magical resolution of problems.[3]

This "holiday syndrome," with its fusion of the pains of passage and pains of season, is reflected in a poem by Mrs. William McCartney Jr., which she sent to me shortly after reading my article "The Pain of Passage" (*Faith at Work,* January 1975).

PASSAGE

We sat together by the lighted Christmas tree,
Bare now of presents
   that were wrapped so festively.
"Mother," she sadly wept,
"Why can't this Christmas last?
I like being little—why
Must I grow old and die?
Why must everything I love change, mother?
   Why?"
What answer could I give
   this child of tender years
When silently my own heart shed unseen tears
For sweet, fleeting moments
   I had yearned to clasp,
Vanished forever from my futile grasp?
For in the wisdom of her innocence and youth,
She had glimpsed the age-old poignant truth
That from the moment each of us is born,
It is the pain of passage that we mourn.

Thus the most gladsome festival we Christians celebrate becomes in the very observing of it a swimming motion by which we acknowledge death in the act of transcending it.

26

TWO

PROCESSES OF DENIAL

Ritual serves as a powerful device for coping with the erosion of time and death. In ritual we are not only given the support of "wise custom," as Lewis claims, but also the presence and steadying influence of the community and the conveying of divine blessing to help us deal with the grief of passage and the anxiety of the unknown.

In most societies the religious system assumes responsibility for ritual. Its representatives, in the persons of priests and other celebrants, give authority and credibility to a ceremony. Obedience to the religious authority and careful observance of the minutiae of the rite thus become conditions for the consolation needed in passage.

Those who profess faith in the God of history, the God of the patriarchs, and the Father of our Lord Jesus, see ritual as something more than this coping strategy. They add a dimension of fulfillment to the rituals of passage and season. They say that nothing in personal or collective history is beyond the power, wisdom, and love of our God. They proclaim that the

27

God of the past is also the God of the present and that passage is God's way of completing his work in us. In celebrations recalling God's acts in human history, believers say with Joseph Sittler, "God has done this once; He will do it again."

But ritual, even that enlivened by the Christian faith, can become a means by which reality is glossed over rather than confronted. The traditional language of the ceremony, once both beautiful and true, becomes after a while only beautiful. The actions of the rite as well as its costuming and spectacle become gradually more ornate and involved, the meaning of the symbolism more remote. Because the ritual symbolizes but is not the passage, the symbol may serve not as a help in passage but as an escape from it. Some years ago on a subway I saw a jingle that says it all. "On Thanksgiving we give thanks, it is the thing to do." "The thing to do," the "handing over to wise custom" of the burden of the passage may deteriorate into merely going through the motions and denying the raw, bleeding edge that passage represents.

When I was serving one of my first parishes, I helped officiate at the funeral of a man to whom I had tried to minister during a long and wearing illness. After the service, I sat with the widow in the family car on the way to the cemetery, giving what support I could in what was for me an overwhelmingly sad situation. I assumed that the mind of the bereaved wife at that moment was filled with only sadness and piety. But as we pulled away from the church, the grieving lady turned to me and whispered, "Please count the cars in the procession. I want John to have a nice funeral."

In my naive idealism, I was shocked by what seemed an insensitive request. How could this woman be concerned about something so crass and quantitative as the number of people who turned out for the funeral? But I have since understood that grief seizes upon many sources of comfort, and that some get through the pain and chaos of loss by counting sympathy cards and floral pieces or by noting how many mourners show up at the wake.

I hope I am now less smug about such things than I used to be and am prepared to give ritual its due. Perhaps the ego esteem that funerals and weddings sometimes provide families is a means of coping with passage. A wedding may serve to bolster the status of the bride and bridegroom's parents and feather the nest of the newlyweds in addition to imparting a divine blessing. And who knows? Perhaps part of the blessing is precisely those signs that appear as material, not to say materialistic, to those who embrace a "higher" set of values.

The tyranny of custom

Twenty years ago, when formal weddings and funerals were still very much *de rigueur* in Sweden, our family was invited to the wedding of a cousin, which was to take place at the ancestral farm. Fortunately we were in Sweden at the time and could accept the invitation. I asked my aunt, the hostess of the celebration, if it would be acceptable if Sally and I came to the wedding in informal dress rather than a long evening dress and white tie and tails. My aunt was deeply affronted. She made me feel that to come to the solemnization without the proper wedding garments would be worse than not coming at all. There was a shop in the next village, she said, whose business it was to rent formal clothes for all occasions. There would be no problem in being outfitted.

I was angered by what seemed to me a tyranny of custom and made the episode an item in my repertoire of mossy country traditions. But I have learned something new about that also. My aunt's demand for conformity in dress was part of her coping mechanism—a way of keeping things in balance by relying on the flywheel of custom. Special wedding garments gave significance to the wedding, lifting it out of the sequence of ordinary tasks, customs, and feelings: the gray meals, the endless washings and sweepings, the routine caresses, exhortations, disciplines, boredoms, and galls of country life.

Rituals help us work through passages, blunting the edge of grief and anxiety and channeling the coursings of joy so we can accept the change that has taken place. But the human heart may, in its flight from painful feelings, develop too much dependence on the machinery of the rite. The symbol is allowed to push away the fact; reality becomes a piece of theater. Thus passage is denied, very much as in late Judaism a relationship with the living Lord may have been denied by meticulous attention to the observances intended to honor him. But a more obvious form of the denial of time and death in our day is the avoidance of ritual altogether, especially ritual suggesting the ultimate.

Recently a woman died in our town. She had willed her body to a prestigious medical school, but her will specified that she wanted no ceremony of any kind to mark her death. Responding to the human need "to do something" about so significant an event as dying, a neighbor, in violation of the woman's wishes, placed a vase of flowers outside the door of the apartment on the day of the woman's death. I am not sure about the propriety of the neighbor's behavior in this situation, although I am confident her motives were benevolent.

Why we avoid ritual

Why do increasing numbers of people avoid ritual? Is it that life is so meaningless that it has no significant moments? Or that the theology underlying ritual has so eroded as to make rites a mockery? Or that the community that gives structure and continuity to existence is too much present in the ritual to make it tolerable? Or is it that ritual, even the most attenuated and routine ritual (the spotted vestments, the wheeze and mumble of the celebrant, the banality of the sanctuary), speaks too powerfully of the reality of passage?

No doubt all of these underlie the present neglect of ceremony, but among them the last seems to be the most telling. We modern Westerners are hysterically afraid of death, and time speaks to us of death and dying. One would think it might be otherwise. The majority of us live longer and more healthily and comfortably than any previous inhabitants of this planet. But it seems that the more of life we have and the better that life is, the more we want of it and the less we are willing to risk it. The media's present discussions of the health hazards in every imaginable product and situation would have been inconceivable to previous generations, which lacked the sophisticated means of detecting such hazards or the ability to avoid them.

The evasion of ritual, which is rooted in fear of passage, ultimately robs life of its solemnity and its deeper joy.[1] Ironically, the number of passages people experience has increased as the use of ceremony to deal with them has decreased. Not only do we now struggle with the passages that time brings; we must also contend with the crises of social and spatial mobility little known a century ago. *Transitional trauma,* one term describing what happens to people who have trouble coping with the tempo and gravity of change, is becoming more and more common in our time.[2]

Transitional trauma affects families experiencing divorce; families of business executives, military and government personnel, and other workers whose jobs keep them on the move; people whose vocational goals have not been reached, who have to lower their expectations; victims of serious financial reverses; those caught in midlife crises; retirees; widows and widowers; and many, many others.

How does the person who no longer finds ritual a

means of coping deal with the trauma of our accelerated life pace? Often by trivializing existence and making it even less meaningful. A spate of magazines — and not just the erotic or pornographic genre—have set about to trivialize sex and sexual relationships. A few years ago, when advocates of "the sexual revolution" began making their onslaughts on a morality that confined genital sexual experience to marriage, the setting for sex was still seen as a "meaningful relationship." Such a condition no longer exists for many in our society. Sexual episodes for their own sake seem taken for granted, and "sleeping around" carries less and less social stigma.

This says that not only has sex been trivialized; the communal matrix which is the source of sexual mores has also been rendered trivial. The community no longer has contact with the "trivializers" or any effective leverage with them. It is hence incapable of providing significant rituals for the passage that overwhelms more and more people.

It is a truism that rituals emerge and develop in community. They reinforce the structures and help to assure the ongoingness of community. Ritual and community thus serve to support each other.

In our time we face a unique phenomenon in history: the opportunity for people to be alone in and independent of the society around them. Society has always had its hermits and recluses, but they have been relatively few and have not indicated a social trend. Today, because of unprecedented financial, social, and perhaps emotional independence, thousands of individuals have been able to abandon the established community, with its disciplines and expectations as well as its consolations. Either they have allied themselves with small countercultural groups or they have chosen to live in solitariness within the *anomie* of the urban beehive.

Primary communities

In the past, primary communities (family, church, school, village or town, and small, intimate work places) provided for the basic needs of individuals, and also for ego esteem and self-actualization (Maslow). People belonged, and they felt secure. These primary communities helped individuals deal with the risks and pains of passage.

Such communities still exist in many places in our world, though their numbers seem to be diminishing. Where it is still effective in the Christian West, the church ushers people into life and community by the rite of Baptism. It signals the onset of puberty by confirming them. It stands by to bless and even to direct their education. It approves vocations and the choice of a marriage partner. It blesses the birth of children and recognizes the service of parents. It enunciates clearly defined standards of behavior. It works to maintain the cohesion and effectiveness of marriage and the family. It is a companion and refuge to the sick, the grieving, the disappointed. Finally, it is ready at the time of aging and death to provide care and solace, as well as transcendent hope.

Persons in such a community ordinarily conform to established values. To assure themselves of the approval and blessing of the church as well as of the larger community, they adapt, suppressing doubts and strong personal inclinations. They may know that the freedom of novel personal choice is available to them, and they may have read the literature of romantic rebellion in which the creative individual is pitted against the tyrannous conservatism of the community, but they choose a less risky and more manageable life-style. In embracing the value system of the church and the related community, they do not see themselves as violating their individual consciences so much as exercising a species of adult self-denial and control for the sake of family and communal stability, and also for the sake of their own sanity and well-being.

By thus solemnizing rather than trivializing life in the community, conforming persons have available to them the celebrative designs of the community to assuage their grief, lessen their anxiety, and intensify their joy. Granted that life can be denied in the midst of celebrating it, the fact nevertheless remains that some vestige of the true solemnity of passage clings to the most banal and perfunctory observance of it.

Even these shreds of meaning elude those who have decided to go it alone. Trivialization becomes a life-style. Not only are marriage and sexual experience made light of, personal relationships are frequently given short shrift. Children are seen as an encumbrance, and relationships to other family members may suffer from neglect, sentimentality, or impulsiveness. After a time, concepts such as faithfulness, devotion, and reliability may go by the board, and whatever meaning life retains is nourished by frequent changes of scene, intense professional or vocational careers, or dramatic mood changers, such as alcohol and drugs.

The loss of community

It is abandonment of community rather than denial of ritual and passage that is the real horror of our time. The latter is only a symbol of the former. Ortega y Gasset may be right in saying that culture and civilization are only convulsive swimming motions used to avoid sinking into the abyss of death. But the fact remains that a swimming body, even in desperation, is still a body in which limbs and lungs, glands and nerves work in concert. It is not a torso or a limb torn loose and bobbing horribly on the seas.

But if community is the body into which we have been created and to which we belong, not out of a primitive need to huddle but as the only field in which it is possible for us to discover and develop our powers, what is to be done in the face of the steady and universal erosion of the communal matrices in which life until now has been nourished, enabled, and disciplined?

On a recent visit to Japan we took the opportunity to visit Buddhist temples, as well as Shinto shrines. In several of them weddings were in progress, or families in their holiday best, from grandparents to babies, were paying a formal visit in search of blessing. We asked knowledgeable friends about these public demonstrations of family solidarity and everywhere got the same answer. The family is still the most cohesive element in Japanese society, but the scene is rapidly changing. In the face of technological and social change, communal values are giving way to private whims and interests. We heard the same story in Russia, even though, since the first giddy days of the revolution were past, the Soviet government has stressed the value of stable family life for national solidarity.

If it is evident that community is essential for human fulfillment, it is equally evident that communities, however desperate the need for them, cannot be formed by mere outward pressures or organizational manipulation. They must be born ultimately from above, more immediately from within; they come into existence as a response to the deepest needs of human personhood. Such communities never correspond exactly to what the human spirit is calling for, for every individual is different. The result is an inevitable tension between the community and the individual, particularly the creative, innovative person who sees farther and wants more than the community can offer.

But despite this tension and the seductiveness of the freedom that calls us to sever our relations with it, the community remains an indispensable part of our lives. Nowhere is this so apparent as in the management of passage, the presiding over the crises of time and death.

It is quite possible that communities as we have known them may give way to the isolating pressures of civilization. Perhaps modern people will believe for a time that they can get along without community, its traditions and ceremonies. But even if this happens, communities will inevitably be reborn, for communities enable us to become what we were created to be.

This book does not speak directly or specifically to the creation of community. What it does seek to envisage is the role of the Christian community as the enabler of our passage through time. The church is seen not only as the custodian of ancient, meaningful ceremonies, but also as the inventor of new ones. It has a vital role in helping individuals assimilate and interpret experience.

The effect of the church's caring service may be renewal of the community, for the essence of community is ultimately people caring for people and being cared for. Hence the fateful choice before us as a people is if we will continue to invest in such caring, or if we will opt for the growing *anomie* of our culture, with both its icy freedom and the ultimate sterility of its isolation.

THREE

THE GAIN AND LOSS OF EDEN

My first tangible, not to say tactile, contact with death came in my fifth year. I had heard of death before: the death of my mother, the death of relatives and neighbors. I had seen death in the upturned belly of a little perch which we caught and tried to keep alive in the basin of the garden fountain. But I first truly experienced death by sharing as an admiring bystander in the burial of a water rat on the shore of our lake.

The celebrants were my older brother and sisters and some other children. They found the cigar box and they made the garlands and dug the hole in the sand. They concocted and led the mumbo jumbo of the burial service. I stood and watched. I remember the soft gray sky, the lake water like mother-of-pearl lapping against the hull of an abandoned boat, and the sense of isolation I felt in the midst of the play—half satire, half solemnity—as my siblings and playmates placed the cigar box in the hole and covered it. It was the same loneliness I felt in passing the churchyard which surrounded the village

39

church and seeing the graves of little children—
no older than I—who had died and gone to be with
Jesus.

Thus I met death and a ritual to deal with it, but
the fear of it never departed. I grew up to fear physical death, the sudden plunge beneath the waves of
which Ortega y Gasset speaks, but I also feared the
death that would diminish me by taking away my
centrality and control. The fear of it was so great
that for many years I would share it with no one.
Thus I shut myself off from the care that my community was ready to provide. It has only been since
I began—reluctantly—to accept that caring that I
have been able to look at death with clearer eyes
and also to assimilate and value the rituals by which
the community seeks to cope with it.

In the pages that follow, I will discuss the meaning of some passages for me, reflect on the meaning
of passage and ritual in the life of Jesus, and suggest ways in which our passages may not only be
celebrated but interpreted and assimilated in the
Christian community.

Grieving over Goldengrove

From the vestiges of the infant scenario that
seem to linger on within us, making every parting
painful, we can assume that all of us felt reluctance
and anxiety about entering the earthly scene. This
pain of primal loss, which seems to figure in every
subsequent experience of separation, is expressed by

Gerard Manley Hopkins in his lyric, "Spring and Fall: To a Young Child":

> Margaret, are you grieving
> Over Goldengrove unleaving?
> Leaves, like the things of man, you
> With your fresh thoughts care for, can you?

The unleaving of Goldengrove—a radical change in the circumstances that have made life bright and happy—underscores the earlier loss of the congenial environment and the unchallenged intimacy of the womb.

The archetype of this state of unbroken blessedness is the situation in the garden of Eden as suggested in the early chapters of Genesis. The Eden story seeks to answer the question: how were things before our relationship to God, to one another, and to the whole of creation became stress-filled and unproductive? In other words, how were things before death? The Eden story says, in effect, this is the way it was, this is a glimpse of the balance between God and persons, between human beings and the rest of creation, and between men and women. That balance was broken by an act of insensitivity toward and cooling regard for the other and by consequent grappling for power.

When Goldengrove unleaves, the deeper sorrow in the loss of the womb and of Eden strikes us. We feel bereft, and in the bereavement there is fear that things will never get better, and that if they don't, we have some share in that. *What have I done now?* That recurring question expresses the guilt all of us feel in the face of loss and grief.

41

Grief accompanies loss

Our four-year-old granddaughter Tessa helps me to see that a child begins very early to struggle with the unleaving of Goldengrove—the pain of passage —both the grief and the anxiety of it. The shopping mall in our town celebrates the holidays by setting up a train for tots. There during the special seasons harried mothers line up with an assortment of moppets, all eager to taste the mystical joy of being railroaded around and around and around. The train ride has become a special delight for Tessa and a relief for her grandfather when storybooks, blocks, crayons, and Sesame Street lose their sparkle.

After Christmas in her third year, when the train, according to custom, was packed up and stowed away, Tessa's mother had the difficult task of telling her that for a time the train had gone "bye-bye." Tessa surprised us by showing no violent signs of impatience or grief. Instead, she was unusually sad and pensive. Then she asked, "Train come back? Train come back soon?" Choking down an impulse to go out and buy her a train on the spot, I assured her it would—sometime. She seemed consoled, but the next time we visited the mall, she broke away from me and went looking in the place where the train had been set up, as if nourishing a hope that, by a miracle, it had already returned.

In Tessa's experience of grief I relive my own childhood feelings—the sense of comfort, coziness, and pleasure in the people, places, and experiences that were a delight to me, and the fear, anxiety, sadness, and perhaps guilt associated with losing them.

My mother died when I was three months old. When I was not yet two, my father remarried. For the next three years my father was gone much of the time. He was involved in the Russian scene, which in the period 1915-18 was far from tranquil, and the family was left in the relative security of Sweden. During these years I developed a very strong dependency on my stepmother, a remarkably gifted and courageous woman, who, at the age of 94, continues to be a most significant person in our life as a family. I recall the acute pain I felt when she was gone from our house even for a short time. We lived on the outskirts of the village, and I remember snowy afternoons when I would stand with my nose pressed against the cold windowpane, staring out into the gathering dusk and trembling with anxiety that she would not come back.

During that time I also became deeply attached to other people and to places and things that suggested security, comfort, and caring. One of our favorite places as children was a farm owned by my grandparents, where an unmarried uncle and aunt continued to live. From my earliest years, the farm, which lay on the other side of a mile of heath and forest, was my "city of refuge." It represented not only the caring of my close kin but the availability of treats of food and drink and a variety of living things, from newborn piglets to bulls, horses, and rams—terrible and glorious beings moving against a background of great beauty.

The farm was my refuge because it relieved me of two pressures. The first pressure was the competitiveness and tension I felt as the runt pig, the youngest of four children. The second pressure was subtler. It was an atmosphere generated by the circle of piety within which we moved in the village. As an adult I have become more aware of the causes of the dourness marking that faith community. Life was meager, burdensome, uncertain, and oriented toward the "other world." It was hence cautious and tentative about this world. Even the valid joys and legitimate excitements of the earth were stamped as frivolous and unstable. One learned in those surroundings to suspect that every apple housed a worm and that every morning blue and bright with promise would end in rain or a worse disaster.

On the farm, life was much less religious, although, for me at least, not less sacred. I found comfort in the daily round of activities: gathering eggs, helping feed the cattle and pigs, harnessing the horses, running errands. I sensed genuine delight in created things: puppies, lambs, colts, calves. There may have been as much anxiety about life on the farm as in the village, but there was less sighing and less biblical footnoting. Hence I felt reassured that it would last longer and that I would not so soon be thrust out of Eden.

But the counterpoint of that security was the realistic awareness that I was, in fact, growing up. The unleaving of Goldengrove was symbolized for me in the progressive shrinking of a small, white, tufted comforter that had always been mine. In the fifth year of my life, I began to notice that it was melting away and becoming less important to me. I wanted to stay that process, to cling to the marvelous softness, but I was also embarrassed by my feelings. Big boys did not treasure such things.

I felt that something lovable and beautiful was vanishing from my life and that I was powerless to stop it. With the passing of the comforter, something of my childhood would pass. I would never again be so much held, so much touched and teased, so much smiled at, cherished, delighted in.

Hopkins ends his lyric with the lines:

> Now, no matter, child, the name:
> Sorrow's springs are the same.
> Nor mouth had, no nor mind expressed
> What heart heard of, ghost guessed:
> It is the blight man was born for,
> It is Margaret you mourn for.

It was indeed Margaret I mourned for—the remembered child in the circle of light and caring, the child who was its own excuse for being and was secure in its identity. It was the child, but it was also Goldengrove. The pain of passage for me was the erosion of the child self, but also the loss of the child-in-relationship, the loss of the circle.

When I was nine we moved far away from the village and from the farm. I came back for many visits, but it was not until 50 years had passed that I could talk to my uncle about the meaning of Goldengrove. We stopped by his little house one day. He was then close to 90, nearly blind and burdened by a stroke, but as bright and merry as he had always been. I said to him, "I want to thank you for what you were for me when I was a very small boy. I understand now that you were my father during the years that he was gone." And he laughed. "Do you remember," he said, "how you would crowd me on the seat of the wagon or sleigh? You couldn't get close enough, and I had to give you a push with my elbow to get room to handle the horses." As we laughed, it was as if this remembering of a relationship had served to celebrate it and to express thanks for it after half a century.

The wound my uncle helped to heal remains open and bleeding for many children. They live in fractured families or rapidly changing situations. They experience privation through the death of a parent, divorce, or a succession of geographical moves, which seem an inevitable part of our social mobility. Each change has in it the pain of passage. If children here experience pain, what must be the trauma of the millions of children who are victims of wars and natural catastrophes?

We may work to reduce instability in the world around us, but there is no hope that, in Blake's grandiose phrase, we shall be able to build "Jerusalem in England's green and pleasant land." There is no return to Eden, no matter how much we learn about the happiness or unhappiness of children. Some experts on the subject of primal pain recommend the Sumerian model of keeping children at the breast for a protracted time, but the anguish of childhood is not significantly assuaged by postponing weaning. The anguish of the man is the anguish of the child. And the anguish of the man is expressed in Francis Thompson's line, "Nature, poor stepdame, cannot slake my drouth." In other words, there is no human way around our fallenness or our mortality. There is only a way through it.

Lost dominions

But the pain of passage involves more than the loss of Eden. It is also present in the encounters of Cain and Abel, Isaac and Ishmael, Jacob and Esau, and Joseph and his many brothers. A scary part of childhood is the shifting and changing of relationships, the trauma of lost thrones and dominions.

Dorothy Sayers tells about her discovery at the age of four that she was a separate person, an *I* over against other *I*s. Young Dorothy found this an exhilarating experience, but for many it also carries pain. To know that I am one helps me to understand other numbers. I may, for example, see that I am no longer indistinguishable from my mother or father, that we are two and may any moment have to adjust to being three. I may have to share my mother with my father or my father with my mother. Thus the conscious rivalry for the place of preeminence begins.

The pain of that experience and its impact on a life is described in Wesley Nelson's book *Crying for My Mother*. It is not a technical or generalized study —Nelson attempts to speak for only his own experience — but it describes the pangs of rivalry and bereavement with considerable power:

47

One day we were out in front of our house when I suddenly realized that my mother had left. She probably just went into the house, but as soon as I missed her, I began as usual to scream for her. My father had grown weary of this endless crying and had begun to chide me for it. This time he said, "Mother is gone. She's tired of your yelling. She's left you for good. She'll never come back." With that, of course, I only screamed louder.

I am sure that my mind would have told me it was not true, but all I could do was feel the weight of his words and the yearning for my mother. By this time I was hysterical.

The fact is that my mother did not come back to me. I am sure that she must have come back and taken me in her arms and comforted me as she always had done before, but that act was blotted from my memory. What my father had said made such an impression on me that I had to make it come true. For years I cried for her. Every time I found myself in difficulty or emotional strain, I had the same frantic feeling I had that day as a boy outside the house when she left for only a few minutes.

By a father or mother or angel, at some point we are ushered out of paradise, even though we may have assumed that we were gods. Some parents hope to behave in such a way as to shelter their children from the tearing loneliness of Oedipus. This is good insofar as it diminishes unhealthy emotional attachments, but unrealistic if it assumes the problem is solvable.

I did my own crying for my mother. When I was two, our stepmother became the mother of us four children in every sense of the word. She was the woman for all seasons, and we lived through all of them with her. Because I was youngest and ill, I got a large share of her attention and care.

According to my mother's reports and some fairly clear memories, I negotiated the position of "little daddy" and on several occasions suggested that my father might stay away and leave me in sole possession of the field. At the ages of two and a half and three, I felt capable of taking care of my mother.

I remember some of this, but I remember more clearly my boisterous resistance when we joined my father briefly in a distant city. We stayed in a modest hotel until more permanent housing would be ready. The suite we occupied had a large sitting room, which was made up in the evening to accommodate the beds of my two sisters and my older brother. Being only three, I was put on the cot in a small bedroom where my parents slept.

I presumably was asleep when my father and mother went to bed, but some sort of unconscious radar must have been at work, for with irritating regularity, night after night, I began to scream the minute their bodies hit the mattress. Out of concern for other guests, or perhaps the tranquility of the community, they would both vault out of bed and run over to my cot to try to modulate my bellow and restore order. In the ancient black and white movie screen of my memory, I can still see their Chaplinesque figures in white nightclothes and hear their voices in a duet of mingled anxiety and desperation punctuated by shushing and feverish whispered commands that I be quiet. Did I hurt? Did I feel hot? Was I frightened? Did I need to go toidy?

My problem was that I felt pushed out of the Eden of exclusive ownership of my mother. I felt

displaced, abandoned, deprived by this bearded
stranger whom I knew only as the abstraction
"papa" and whose rights to claim my mother's presence I did not understand and was certainly not
ready to accept.

Children's sense of displacement

Giving up dominion to my father threatened to
diminish me, but as the youngest I escaped another
kind of pain of intrusion: the birth of a younger
brother or sister who draws away the attention of
one's parents to a new and alien being. I have seen
the hurt of that event in the faces of older children.
Adults seem to find the pain of that passage humor-
ous, but to the affected child it is far from funny. It
is possible to see the scars of displacement in the
faces of brothers and sisters at family reunions
when the battles of the nursery are six or seven
decades past.

I use the word *displacement* advisedly. I am aware
that most parents do not consciously desire to push
one child away in favor of another. I believe that
parents are truthful when they assure me, as they
often do, that they try to treat their children equita-
bly. But that is not my point. I happen to believe
that such equity is a fiction, but in this instance the
problem is not that of the parents so much as of the
child. The child who has worked through some of
the trauma of the triangle—mummy and me and
daddy or daddy and me and mummy—and may feel

50

some security with both parents must now make room for a pretender to the throne.

The interest that an older child takes in a newborn may conceal deeper feelings of resentment and envy than we sometimes associate with a well-adjusted child. Freud talks about little children who dream of their brothers and sisters as angels. (In other words, "I wish they'd fly away.") Even the Bible, especially the Old Testament, makes no effort to pretty up the feelings of one sibling toward the other. Cain and Abel is an extreme case, but Ishmael and Isaac, Jacob and Esau, Joseph and his brothers, and the pugnacious and treacherous sons of David all suggest the difficulty of seeing brothers and sisters as friends rather than as intruders and adversaries.

My father, who had difficulties with his own siblings, used to agonize over his children's teasing and fighting. We did not take our squabbling too seriously, but he, perhaps more aware than we of the hostility lurking under the surface in every family, used to quote the words of Joseph to his brothers: "Don't quarrel on the way."

I may not have made my father's eyes sparkle, to borrow Myron Madden's phrase, but I was my mother's blessed child. I have been slow in my awareness of the pain that must have brought to my siblings— the pain of seeing an interloper occupying the throne and the pain of feeling thereby diminished.

The deeply hid hostility arising from the feeling of displacement does not make affection among siblings impossible or even rare. Adult siblings are often good friends. They carry shared images. They belong to a community of history and tradition and perhaps of values. But when the childhood scene is reenacted or simulated, the old hostilities may surface. That is why family reunions, especially those that last longer than a day, are often such bleak affairs. They are a process of "show and tell" played out before parents, or at least the tribe. Siblings with their children and spouses, like Esau and Jacob in the presence of Isaac, are all looking for the blessing, and some, like Jacob, are willing to play games to get it.

I was amused and surprised when one of our daughters-in-law recently reported her impressions of our last reunion as an entire family. I could not believe what she and others perceived in my behavior toward our children. I had made every effort to be just and equitable, but apparently I failed, for the siblings and their spouses amused themselves by pointing out ways in which my behavior toward them was far from impartial.

On last Father's Day the Sunday papers carried statements by several eminent Americans of their feelings about their fathers. I was struck by the uniformly laudatory sound of these statements. There was not a hint of the awkwardness that, despite my respect and affection for my father, always characterized our relationship.

As Dean Inge once said, "One should not make fun of people while they are at their devotion," and I do not want to discredit the almost pious air that hung over these Father's Day tributes. The words

certainly sounded sincere. Some of them nevertheless also sounded like verbal "tribute" in the original
sense of that word. They were tributes made to
living and dead fathers in such a way as to fend
off the claim of rival and intrusive loves. I wonder
if the tributes said not only "Thanks, Dad" but also
"How could you ever doubt that I love you more than
all of them and thus deserve to inherit the kingdom?"

The Game of One

The numbers game of which children become
aware, if only dimly, may lead at some point to the
Game of One. The pain of being a loner may seem
less than the pain of the group. Relationships bring
fear of shame and rejection, fear of cloying dependency. Loners avoid the risk of being diminished,
the sense of failed expectations that a broken relationship brings.

Ordinarily, solitude is good. Creative withdrawal
provides respite from the demand to "make it." I
can discover the delight of me and the joy of irresponsibility quite apart from everyone else. The
person who cannot enjoy such solitude but must
cram it full of images and voices and people and
activities, real or piped in by radio or TV, is probably emotionally undernourished. Without some creative solitude, I probably don't know who I am or
who God is.

At my childhood refuge of the farm, I could be
present to myself and absent from older siblings,
whose expectations I could not meet, and from

adults, who sometimes jammed my receiver. I delighted in the farm animals, who asked little of me and who gave me nothing except the delight of their presence. The human beings in the refuge also let me be. They told me stories, but they spared me a lot of teaching. I was to discover later that most of us get too few stories and too many lessons.

But to be alone in that way and to be a loner are different things. After observing myself over a period of years, I can perceive the difference between the me who, while feeling OK about himself, chooses to be apart for rest, relaxation, meditation, prayer, creative work, or creative indolence, and the not-OK me who, driven by who-knows-what guilts, shames, fears, or hurts, crawls, like a sick animal, into solitariness. The latter is the Game of One.

The test, I think, is how rhythmic the pattern is, how much freedom I have to move from world to world. Solitariness as a permanent flight from reality cannot be good. It has the power to flatten and depersonalize us.

The artistic personality, whose art is nourished from within quite as much as from without, probably needs "the place apart" more than we ordinary mortals. In that context we understand Elinor Wylie's harsh injunction:

> Shun the polluted flock,
> Live like that stoic bird
> The eagle of the rock.

But permanent solitariness violates a cardinal principle in our nature. Solitude that shuns the risk and pain as well as the consolation of relationship is self-destructive. It is no accident that Dante, who lived for years in galling and lonely exile from Florence, saw that one of the horrors of the Inferno is solitariness. Even in the first circle, where lust draws people together in a grisly community, there is at the heart only revulsion and aloneness.

In motivating the creation of woman in Genesis, God said, "It is not good that the man should be alone; I will make him a helper fit for him." *Helper* may be interpreted to mean "obedient servant," but the dynamic of the creation story belies that meaning, for Eve is Adam's companion. Companionship, relationship, community—not isolation—is our end.

In sketching the most primitive of Christian doctrines of the "last things," Paul writes, "Then we who are living at that time will be gathered up along with them in the clouds to meet the Lord in the air. And so we will always be with the Lord. So then, encourage one another with these words" (1 Thess. 4:17-18 TEV). This promise of beloved community is unquestionably the way things ought to be and will be.

FOUR

THE WORLD ALL BEFORE THEE

The concluding lines of Milton's *Paradise Lost* state the problems and the promise of our first parents as they leave Eden behind. They also describe the experience of children growing toward adulthood:

> Some natural tears they dropped
>   but wiped them soon;
> The world was all before them, where to choose
> Their place of rest, and Providence their guide:
> They hand in hand
>   with wandering steps and slow,
> Through Eden took their solitary way.

The polarity of our human existence—the comfort of security and the excitement of choice—breaks in upon children the moment they are old enough to sense:

1. that they are separate persons;
2. that there is a world outside the family;
3. that there are optional ways of responding to things.

The pain of passage for children is the grief of leaving Eden behind. The delicious sense of being cared for and having limited responsibility for myself gives way to the anxiety of stepping into a situation where I am responsible for me and have to trust more and more to my own resources.

This scenario is repeated throughout our lives. We are often forced to choose whether to stay with the familiar or risk the strange. Are we conservatives or liberals, settlers or pioneers, servants of the establishment or entrepreneurs?

I spent five years in the military service, some of it in combat. During that time I learned what it meant to be terribly alone and left to my own desperate choices. I also experienced the seductiveness of being almost totally cared for. I recall my sense of security when we embarked for the European Theater in World War II. Almost every detail of the long trip by troop train and troop ship was someone else's responsibility. We were fed, clothed, transported, instructed, inspired, and even entertained by the U.S. Army, without having to make any major choices. This carefree time was a fitting prelude to the existential terror of being alone with our own dying and with the choice of whether to flee or to stand.

The trials of puberty

The alternations between security and risking, between the coziness of the communal hive and the exhilaration and anxiety of flying solo, start early and continue late. But they are particularly present in the zone between child and adulthood we call puberty, when physiological and psychic changes force the issue.

A measure of the difficulty is indicated by the root meaning of the word *puberty*. It signifies the time of the emergence in both sexes of what we call secondary gender characteristics—the appearance of body hair, for example. Physical changes provide evidence that there is no escape route into the past. From that stage on we are committed to being adults.

The sexual revolution has sent shock waves of sexual awareness into the world of children. Under such stimulus, many children cannot wait to become sexually active. But hastening such desire does not lessen the pain of passage. When the fevers of premature sexuality and commitment have subsided, many feel deep nostalgia for the childhood that cannot be recalled.

Some years ago, when the need for sex education in the lower grades was becoming a hot political issue, I began informally checking out what young people remembered about the onset of puberty and what their dominant feelings were at that time. Most of them confessed to being ignorant about some sexual facts and feeling anxious about that. Most felt that the information their parents provided was inadequate and was conveyed in such a way as to make both parties embarrassed. Most of them tended to agree that sex education introduced as part of a general life science program in the schools may have been factually helpful.

But for many, the troublesomeness of puberty was not ignorance or confusion so much as grief—the grief of passage. The appearance of sex characteristics—the onset of menstruation in girls and of involuntary seminal emissions in boys—even when they knew the facts, was an experience of genuine sorrow. It was also, of course, an experience of excitement and hope, a sense of standing at the boundary of a country promising new experience.

But this did not rule out the sorrow. For most of them, puberty spelled the end of childhood and hence of undifferentiated play. In childhood girls could climb trees and play ball; boys could be accepted as equal partners in "girl games." I know there is now strong pressure to play down these differences so girls can play ball and boys can dress dolls as long as they like, but that is hardly my point. It is rather that, at some time, because of the fact of passage, children become adults. With that change comes a gradual end to the choicelessness and spontaneity and the sense of being cared for, and an entering of the world of decision and accountability quite different from childhood. And this is sad.

Fear of dying

With the onset of puberty comes also an awareness of being left alone with one's own fear of dying. As a child of seven I was taken to a provincial hospital in southern Sweden for treatment of an acute infection requiring surgery. Because my family lived many miles away, I had to spend the time following my operation alone at the hospital. Those were the days before the sulfa drugs and antibiotics, and I was surrounded by gravely ill and dying children.

I was afraid of death, and I was happy when I was finally dismissed from that community of pain. But I was sustained by the faith of my mother and of Sister Martha, a Christian nurse on my ward. The night before surgery, when Sister Martha came by my bed to share my evening prayer, she asked me if I was ready to die and go to be with Jesus. It seemed quite natural to say that I was. I did, of course, hope that the matter might have another issue, but in my own childish way I was ready to trust.

But adolescence was another matter. I felt during my terrible struggles with doubt and anxiety that I was totally alone. An unbelievable hypochondriac, I fretted about every possible disease and infirmity and actually induced some cardiac irregularity by my worry. Behind the somber shapes of illness I glimpsed the awesome presence of death. I no longer feared, as in my childhood, the sudden apocalyptic end of my universe, but I struggled with the finality of physical death.

With convulsive swimming motions I tried to keep my head above the surface by steeping myself in literature that promised personal immortality. I read the Bible, the more comforting part of Cicero, Milton, Tennyson, Browning, S. Parkes Cadman, and Henry van Dyke. And I tried my own hand at writing poetry and essays promising hope. I believed for a time that I could assure my survival if I were ready to give up my life in service and suffering, and I embarked on a path of unblessedness, which I have described elsewhere.

Beneath all this turbulence the conviction grew that I was now totally responsible for myself, and this feeling was supported by several abortive attempts to get help with my fears and doubts from my father, whom I admired greatly. For whatever reason, he had no word that reached down into my existential despair, and I was left to swim alone.

Demands of the adolescent body

This was particularly true when it came to the struggle with my changing body and its insistent demands. Not only was I becoming more physically awkward, sown with *acne vulgaris*—O happy term —and presented with surprises such as body hair, I was also beset by cravings I could neither understand nor satisfy. The exalted morality of Tennyson's Galahad and St. Agnes gave imagery to the repression in which I lived, but under that Victorian tranquility, another breed of creature grinned and growled.

In *Portrait of the Artist as a Young Man,* James Joyce puts some of these struggles into the character of Stephen Dedalus:

> As he stared through the dull square of the window of the schoolroom, he felt his belly crave for its food. He hoped there would be stew for dinner, turnips and carrots and bruised potatoes and fat mutton pieces to be ladled out in thick peppered flour-fattened sauce. "Stuff it into you," his belly counseled him.

Oh, that counsel of the belly! How it tore at the spider web of my ideals! I seemed to have a menagerie of hungry animals somewhere below the navel. In the midst of grandiose fantasies such as jumping over trees, delivering sermons in deathless prose to crammed cathedrals, writing better poetry than Rupert Brooke or Lord Tennyson, dying heroically in an effort to stamp out bubonic plague, or pitching the Pittsburgh Pirates single-handedly through the World Series, I saw my lofty ego the victim of my own animal—a cross between Lucifer and an ape—sinking at last into the primordial muck.

What I felt at those times was a sense of having failed not only Sir Galahad and St. Agnes, but all the people who believed in me. And, of course, when they knew all about me, I would be pushed out of the temple of holiness and made to join the outcasts who sat in the untidy forecourt wailing and gnashing their teeth.

There was, of course, grace, but for me it was a homiletic abstraction available to believing Christians only in small doses, like the grape juice doled out in communion glasses or the crumb of bread accompanying it. I did not trust the grace my father talked about. To me it was like those frail bridges of rope thrown across Burmese chasms, which seem incapable of sustaining their own weight.

There was one exception. The interim pastor of our church was an aging man, stooped and seamed and not entirely put together. He carried a sorrowing grace in his eyes. One day he asked when I was going to share in my first Communion. "I am not worthy to commune," I said. "I am not like the others here." He looked at me out of those eyes that seemed mysteriously "acquainted with grief," and he said the word I did not expect to hear: "None of use here is worthy to commune. Communion isn't that sort of thing."

Taking responsibility for oneself

But the guilt, estrangement, and loneliness of my animality were only part of the pain of adolescent passage. A large part of it was the sense of having fewer and fewer places where I could be spontaneous and irresponsible. One day on the eve of my freshman year in high school, my father called me into the dining room, where he often sat after supper studying or writing. He announced to me somewhat abruptly that since I was now no longer a child (I was 14) I would henceforth be totally responsible for myself. He would no longer tell me what to do or not to do.

To those who deplore the overprotectiveness of some parents toward their children, my father's pronouncement may seem to indicate a high trust in my ability to decide things for myself. This was undoubtedly his intention. But at a very deep level I felt it an act of rejection. He sat looking intently at his unfobbed pocket watch (he usually held it between the fingers of both hands as if it were a chalice), and he sounded angry. He may have been frightened. But I thought I heard that he no longer wanted the chore or risk of being my father and caring for me.

That is not fair to him. Many of his actions toward me spoke of love and concern, and at least once he forgot himself entirely and impulsively snatched away the freedom he had given me. But the test for me is that I remember that conversation with pain. I had some sense of the sweet giddiness of freedom, but I had a deeper feeling of not mattering. My older brother seemed to matter more. I was assured that, like the elder brother in the parable, I had the right of my father's presence and my portion of the inheritance, but what I wept for was the gift of the Prodigal—not so much the fatted calf and the new shoes and the ring on the finger, although a party now and then may have helped, but the opportunity to weep out my anxiety, my grief, my guilt, and my shame in the circle of my father's care.

There was, of course, a different side to my nature. I was impatient with restrictions and intoxicated by the new ideas, feelings, and experiences available to me. In thinking back, I see that I wanted both the warmth and security of childhood and the freedom to make my own choices. I did not want to be a rebel, for I respected and really needed the moral and spiritual values of my parents, but I wanted the right and the opportunity to explore options with them. By putting me so entirely on my own, my father was denying me both the opportunity to ease out of that in my childhood which needed to be left behind and an equally meaningful opportunity to hammer out my values on the anvil of his wisdom and experience.

I do not want to be hypercritical about my father's handling of the situation, for we make most of our mistakes because we're afraid. When my turn came to be the parent of adolescent children, I made similar mistakes. I did not see clearly enough that children in transition want limits, a solid brick wall to bounce their uncertainties against, while at the same time they want freedom to challenge the wall. I was afraid to be too definite in the limits I set down for fear the children would end up not liking me, but I was also afraid to enter into long debates with them on the validity of my system. I feared that they might be right. And, of course, they too were afraid.

I remember a conversation with one of our sons who was then in his late teens. We were driving through the country, amicably discussing the aesthetics of Nietzsche, when, for the first time in my experience, he pulled out a pipe and tobacco pouch and began to smoke. "I need to do this," he said, and puffed away with enviable coolness.

My instant reply was, "I understand that and it's OK." I think I was going to add, "So long as you stay away from cigarettes," but thought better of it. He surprised me by getting angry and saying, "I don't want you to understand and I don't want you to think it's OK. I need to have you disagree." He was saying that the function of parents is to furnish those dictums which provide the pleasure and the learning of transgression.

A new generation

Relationships are complicated during the transitional time of adolescence, and never in our history as a people have peer relationships been more important or more risk-filled than now. They seem to start earlier, because of preoccupied parents, and they are more serious. The shift of focus from one's family to one's own age group—which should theoretically be a normal and natural process—now carries a nightmarish risk not dreamed of a generation or two ago. The risk is that our children may be seduced or even coerced into destructive and irreversible behavior. It is one thing to have the Prodigal Son return home from the carousing and the harlots wisened and saddened; it is something else to have him carted home without a chance of recovery.

A generation or two ago, before the advent of the Pill and the drug scene, many Americans' adolescence was not unlike Eugene O'Neill's portrayal of it in *Ah, Wilderness!* The risks to which young people may then have been drawn by their peer group were those of unwanted pregnancy, too much alcohol, or venereal disease. Serious as these were, they did not begin to compare with the unrelieved tragedy of hard-drug addiction and related criminal behavior. The prevailing mood of many young victims today is no longer Promethean defiance but rather helplessness, as if they are praying for a miraculous rescue which they know cannot come.

It would be arrogant to presume to understand what motivates young people to follow such a clearly marked course to self-destruction. I can only look at them from the perspective of my own personal history. As an adolescent I longed for such a jumble of things that I am surprised ever to have made any sense of it, but my deepest motive was to stay *alive*, with freedom to be my own person, but not so much freedom as to be cast loose from my moorings in God or in my family, especially my father. I took my stable relationship with my mother for granted and had no fear of losing her, but I felt no such security in relation to my father.

Life was precious to me, and I cast around for whatever lifesavers or life rafts were available. Perhaps the very limits within which my pietist culture forced me to live made existence sweeter, much as chastity endows erotic love with an almost intolerable delight. But deeper than day-to-day life was life itself, the primal, physical process of breath and pulse and sensory messages, to which I clung and which I wished to protect.

So much did I cherish that life that I was willing to embark on any pilgrimage to retain it. I now believe that my decision midway in my high school career to become a pilgrim, crusader, martyr, monk, missionary, savior—the purposive sufferer, in other words—was a trade-off I was willing to make to keep my life, or at least my ego, intact.

In this naive vision and purpose, I had the support of my church culture and, with some reservation, my family. But I also had a wealth of literary and historical models, a procession of pure and devoted heroes, from the Christians in the arena through

Richard the Lion-Hearted, the Swedish kings from Engelbrekt to Charles XII, and others such as Father Damien, Arthur Jackson, Wilfred Greenfell, and Florence Nightingale.

I did not then understand that these dear people were human like myself and had their own ambitions and anxieties to struggle with. Nor did I understand myself well enough to see that what appeared noble in me was at the heart of it neither noble nor ignoble, but almost instinctive: the price I would pay to stay alive and perhaps in control.

In this I now see myself the brother of the young people all around me struggling in their way to stay alive within the drug culture. They are moving their arms in a convulsive swimming motion, just as I did. But they have chosen or had chosen for them an element to swim in that will not sustain them for very long. Their flailing is a flailing in quicksand, and those around them cannot help.

I am not wise enough to know what the solution to this problem is, and I do not feel parental or patronizing in talking about it. What I think I feel is empathy with those who are where they are. Perhaps when they made their choices their models were different from mine or the community to which they had entrusted themselves cared less than mine did. Perhaps, too, if they submit to rescue, they will understand better than I did or do what miracle is, the unconditional charity that asks nothing more of us than the opening of a door.

FIVE

TO CHOOSE

The pain of adolescence comes and goes, but never disappears entirely. Part of it is submerged and lives on within us to break out in later life in attitudes and behavior that both trouble and delight us. During the recent revival of interest in the psychology of Jung, several people told me how they came to an understanding of their own adolescence and early maturity and became aware of how much of their past was still with them.

But the entrance into adulthood is a passage marked by its own jumble of feelings.

> We look before and after,
> And pine for what is not;
> Our sincerest laughter
> With some pain is fraught.

Shelley's words can be applied to adolescence but are equally true of the threshold of adulthood.

For purposes of discussion we shall assume that in our culture the entrance into adulthood takes place with graduation from high school. Dependence on the family continues, to a degree, but after high school young people are left relatively free to choose their life direction. They are probably many years away from achieving emotional adulthood, but they are assumed to be responsible, and responsibility is the essence of adulthood.

There are some obvious exceptions to this rule. In religiously conservative communities, parental control seems to continue longer. Some evangelical Christian colleges continue to function *in loco parentis* and consider it their contractual obligation to duplicate the disciplines and controls of the well-regulated Christian family. The reasoning seems to be that high school graduates are not mature enough to make their own decisions and they continue to need a protective environment.

The chaos among young adults seems to argue for such a parental attitude, but the trend is certainly not in that direction. The great popularity of Bill Gothard's seminars, in which he pleads for larger doses of parental authority and greater submissiveness among children, probably signals not so much a trend toward conservatism as the insecurity of parents who cannot cope with growing freedom among their young people.

Making decisions

The transition to adulthood usually issues out in a decision to continue one's education at a college or university, to pursue a vocation, perhaps with supportive vocational training, and, quite apart from these, to marry or not to marry. However, the situation is changing in these as in many other areas. A few years ago the assumption was that every able-bodied male would serve in the military and that every qualified young adult would go on for training beyond high school. But military service is no longer mandatory, and the assumption "the more education, the better" is being challenged because of the lack of employment opportunities for the highly qualified.

There is also growing distaste for the work for which higher education is a preparation. In the upper Michigan area where we spend a great deal of our leisure summer time, there are six college-trained young men who are not working at the vocation for which their years on campus qualified them. They are busy with a number of things, including camp leadership and carpentry, and they seem socially productive and personally fulfilled. Hence, despite the recent push by the NEA and related agencies for a minimum of two years of college, some young people are opting for earlier entrance into the vocational world.

But whatever the choices, college, work, and marriage are all systems in which continuity, commitment, and a certain quality of performance are expected.

Being considered competent for a career and for marriage brings ego satisfaction, but this transitional time may be filled with grief and anxiety and even tinged with anger and depression. Young adults may feel thrust out of Eden, bereft of the freedom, gladness, irresponsibility, and high jinks that are

71

part of youth. They may, in fact, see their new adult responsibilities as a repetition of the dreary fate of Adam and Eve: "You shall gain your bread by the sweat of your brow until you return to the ground" (Gen. 3:19 NEB).

Loss of personal identity

The young person confronted with society's awesome systems is aware that each of them requires the partial subordination of individual identity to the collective. At least, the systems' payoffs depend on such subordination. Hence, while being an adult may guarantee some control of one's life, it does not offer the heady freedom young people sometimes dream of.

The crux of the matter is personal identity. In simpler societies, at least those with humane values, it may be easier to retain one's identity within the community. The rural scene or village or town seems to develop behavioral consonance (or perhaps uniformity) without the destructive loss of selfhood. On the other hand, small communities do impose restrictions. Flaubert, Maupassant, Zola, Hardy, and other 19th-century novelists seem to delight in portraying the bondage of country life, in reaction against the country romantics.

Whatever the truth of that country mouse–city mouse distinction, the modern technological community, with its emphasis on interchangeable parts and people and its stress on profitability, gives the individual, as a self-determining organism, less and less significance.

Sally and I live most of the year in a relatively small community, but we are already being drawn into a banking system that is on the way to being completely automated. To draw money from the bank, we simply insert a secret number and a plastic bank card into a computer, indicate the amount of money we need by pressing some buttons, and presto! the transaction is complete (that is, when it doesn't malfunction like other vending machines).

The implication of this for Sally and me is that we mean less and less as people. Money is issued to us solely on the basis of our computerized record. There is no face-to-face encounter, no buildup of open-ended trust, no allowance for human frailty, and certainly no creative affirmation. Put in another way, it is a community of law, not of grace and acceptance.

I do not argue with the bank's action, for it is dictated by a need for greater efficiency and economy and by the erosion of personal honesty in our society. I only deplore the inevitable lowering of the human temperature that such a change carries with it. Even banks with people in them have not been known for exaggerated friendliness, although we all know some exceptions, but this will make a visit to the bank like going into a meat locker.

Young people required to live in a world of role determination, where personal identity and creativity seem to mean less and less, may hesitate to give their nonworking day to organizations resembling their working world. Many families, churches, and communities offer only minor variations of what they find in their jobs. We may well ask how the roles of the adaptive spouse, parent, church member, church or community leader differ from the roles played at the office.

And the more we are pushed into roles and away from our personhood, the less alive we feel. It is as if we are no longer accessible to the Holy Spirit, the giver of life. We fear this kind of death, the diminishing and perhaps fading out entirely of our beleaguered self among the vast impersonal galaxies of computers—computers managed by computers.

The popularity of *Star Wars* must lie in its recovery of old half-forgotten feelings, such as devotion and heroism, and in the warming up and humanizing of some of the computers. Delightfully scuffed and shabby, these humanized computers and robots serve as friends and allies of the "good guys." They help us remember how good it is to be in a band of brothers and sisters who share their frailty and their apprehensions in what often seems a hopeless quest, and how much safer we feel with persons than with all our shiny hardware.

My first plunge into university graduate school was not an entirely happy experience. I found many of my professors too frightened or preoccupied to see me as a person, and I went through some bad years in which I felt psychologically hazed by people who I later discovered were threatened out of their skulls by both colleagues and students. But their neglect or hostility was not personal. There were,

74

fortunately, others who believed that working with students was their primary vocation, and because of them I endured. So my own entrance into the adult world, scary as it was, was warmed by some happy circumstances.

The rebellions of youth

I am indebted to Bruno Bettelheim in understanding another aspect of my entrance upon the adult scene. During the difficult days of student unrest in the late '60s or early '70s, Bettelheim wrote that today's students were fortunate to have the opportunity to protest. When he was a student in the '30s, he explained, jobs were so difficult to get and to keep that very few people would have dared to jeopardize their job security by expressing their discontent about anything. That describes my own situation. I tended, with my friends and coworkers, to be conformist out of grim necessity.

A friend, aware of the negative reactions of some of his contemporaries toward the modern established community, is working with Gail Sheehy's concept of "Catch 30." He believes that arriving at age 30 constitutes a signal for him and other adults in his age bracket to turn their backs on the "cities of destruction"—the Babylons and Romes of the 20th century, with their hard programs and their predictable expectations for people—and to enter upon a risky wilderness wandering, which promises greater freedom and greater fulfillment for the individual.

A significant social history might be written about how in previous centuries other masses of young people have felt similar urges. The monastic movements of the fourth century were energized essentially by young people. These movements called thousands of Christian sisters and brothers from the corruptions and temptations of metropolitan life and from a devitalized church to the solitude and austerity of the desert.

Another example of such wilderness wanderings is the massive immigration of the last century in which millions of young people left the stability of their European homeland for the risk and promise of America. It is true that for most of the immigrants the intolerable social and economic situation in their home countries provided motivation for leaving home, but for countless others, adventure, freedom, and the promise of the new land lured them forth.

This is not the place to analyze the motivations underlying such choices and actions, but for many young people the exodus from modern life may be fueled by nostalgia for the lost Atlantis of youth, the lost paradise of relative simplicity and beauty where life was not "seared with trade; bleared, smeared with toil" (Hopkins), and where they had some significance as persons.

The churches have traditionally encouraged young adults to enter a responsible vocation and to establish a stable marriage and family life. If more and more young people are opting out of such vocations and out of traditional family life, the question must be raised how their new life-styles square with classical Christian norms. We shall return to this question when we consider the church's responsibility and opportunity in relation to the young adult.

SIX

THE MIDDLE YEARS— AND THE END

The pain of passage does not end with marriage or the entering upon a career or even with a less traditional choice. Our early life is so crowded with demands and expectations, so burdened with preparation—learning, habituation, routine, discipline— that we want to believe the fairy-tale ending "they lived happily ever after." We want to believe that when school is over, courtship is over, looking for a job is over, military service is over, and our debt paid, anxiety also will be a thing of the past and we can live tranquilly in our "blue heaven." Let there be a time, we pray, when the plot is resolved, the bad punished and the good rewarded, the fire covered, the lights put out, and the risk and pain over and done with.

But, of course, there is no such time. Adults may be shamed into repressing some of their pain and even believe that turmoil belongs mainly to youth, but every stage of adulthood has its own discomfort and tension as well as its own delight. Passages seem not to diminish but to multiply as we grow older, and the need to choose remains with us.

Many of us move up the ladder of family life. Our children are born, move through the turbulence of childhood, become settled into their school routines, grow to womanhood and manhood, are married, and, in turn, beget. We become grandparents almost imperceptibly, caught in Yeats' "sensuous music" of "whatever is begotten, born, and dies."

We finish our preparation for a career and begin to pursue it. We formulate goals or have them formulated for us. We may remain geographically static and work our way up the wobbly ladder to the top within a single town, or we may become journeymen for corporations, moving more frequently than migratory birds. But whatever our route, we do not avoid the risk of choice and the pain of passage.

There is a passage in failing—being promoted to the highest level of one's incompetence—but there is also a passage in succeeding. We are lifted up above our brothers and sisters and feel their admiration; we also feel their resentment and envy. Something has happened to the old dynamic: the genial collegiality, the easy interaction. We may plead that we have not changed, but something has changed. Young Joseph preening himself in the bright feathers of his dream may be insensitive to what his brothers are feeling. But Joseph as Pharaoh's aging, balding quartermaster with a thickening waist and a troublesome squint, knows the loneliness of eminence. There may be room at the top, but it has a price tag.

Even so, the most painful passage of middle years

79

may be when we no longer believe that achievement has real significance. To sit at Pharaoh's right hand may be an impossible dream at 17; at 37 or 47 or 57 I may have achieved it but it may not be what I expected. Some of that disillusionment compounds the bitterness of the men who surrounded Richard Nixon.

Surrendering one's roles

The climbing up is painful. So much is left behind, and it cannot be reclaimed. The descent may be even more painful. The rash King Lear, eager to be freed from the burdens of his realm, moves to divide his kingdom among his three daughters. He tells his startled court:

> Know we have divided
> In three our kingdom; and 'tis our fast intent
> To shake all cares and business from our age,
> Conferring them on younger strengths, while we
> Unburdened crawl toward death.

But life offers no such "unburdened crawling" to anyone, and, in Shakespeare's mind, especially not to a king. Searching for freedom from care, Lear loses his identity.

No matter how carefully we prepare for the passage into old age and its related pain, we seem never to be quite ready for what we find. To cease being a young man or young woman of great promise, to cease being parent and provider, to become the old man, old prexy, professor emeritus, senior elder, senior hostess, grande dame, grand old man of Senate, bar, or bench—all this, whatever its benefits in terms of release of tension, in terms of veneration and gratitude, is touched with pain. Cicero, harassed and rendered anxious by a turbulent political career, could write serene paragraphs about old age in his *De Senectute,* but he knew little about aging from experience.

The energies that once embarrassed us by their presence and perhaps by their fullness now humiliate us by their absence. We may try to fool ourselves about diminishing strength, but other people defer to it. They help us with our luggage and find us a chair.

In puberty we said a tearful good-bye to the security of being cared for and not having to make decisions. Now this state of dependence reappears, and we resent it. My aging father (he lived to be almost 94) said that for him the bitterest text in the Bible was Jesus' word to Peter by the Sea of Galilee: "When you were young, you used to get ready and go anywhere you wanted to; but when you are old, you will stretch out your hands and someone else will tie you up and take you where you don't want to go" (John 21:18 TEV).

That is now an experience close enough for me to understand a little of its pain.

The final parting

Partir, est mourir un peu says a French proverb— "To part is to die a little." To age is also to die a little, or to die little by little. The swimming motion that has kept us at the surface of the water loses its vigor and we face in a starker form Job's melancholy reflection, "We are all born weak and helpless. All lead the same short, troubled life. We grow and wither as quickly as flowers; we disappear like shadows" (14:1-2 TEV).

Because life, despite its troubles, is sweet, the prospect of departing from it is repugnant. During past centuries, Christians have been morbidly preoccupied with the topic of death, but the faith itself affirms life. Even our Lord, although he anticipated his own death, did not like it and wanted to avoid it. Unlike Keats, he was not "half in love with easeful death."

Recently, because of Elisabeth Kübler-Ross's brilliant analysis of the processes of death and dying, there has been a great deal of clinical interest in the topic. Many people have been helped to cope with the death of loved ones and the resultant grief process as well as with thinking about their own death. Two or three years ago in our own community a series of workshops about death drew large, interested crowds. Many who attended were young people who may not have thought much about the subject of death. Like many other unpleasant things in our culture, death has been cosmetized beyond recognition, both by the funeral process and by our rhetoric.

But to attend seminars on death and dying and finish off the evening with a cheeseburger and a beer is not the same as to die. Even to cope with someone else's death is not to die. In fact, knowing more and more about death may blind us to its actual pain. For knowledge about something is a form of control. It is, in fact, one of the "swimming motions." And dying is the final relinquishment of control. To die fully is to hand the control for me and my circumstances over to others and ultimately to God. It is the process of surrender pushed to its extreme.

My inordinate fear of death and dying is probably because of this loss of control. I have surrounded my departing with a lot of rhetoric, but that probably represents more what I would like to have happen than what it will be like. I have told myself that the death process will be analogous to submitting myself to general anesthesia and major surgery, but that analogy is false. I have willingly submitted to surgery and have taken pride in being a good patient, calm and relaxed, stoically baring my arm to the needle and waving a benign farewell to the bystanders.

But to die may be to go unwillingly and without the dignity of a Thomas More or the gallant defiance of Mary, Queen of Scots. It may be to be struck down like an ox, without time and opportunity for composure. (I saw a heifer slaughtered when I was not more than seven, and it was unbelievably horrible.) Or it may be to fade imperceptibly into the confusion of dotage or to snore away in a coma. How will I, who have maintained control in everything—except perhaps delirium, nightmares, accidents, diarrhea, and vomiting—how will I feel about having to let go like that? I don't know. But I suspect that death is such a thing. For most of us it will be giving up our weapon, raising our hands above our heads, and stumbling across the border into whatever awaits us on the other side.

I don't know how it will be or how I will behave, but I pray for two things. The first is the courage to face *reality*. It may be a terrible thing to fall into the hands of the living God, but it is also a comfort to cling to that rock of incorruptible truth. The second thing I pray for is help. I know that we die alone, but I am going to need help.

What the implications of these prayers are I shall try to develop in what follows.

PART II

JESUS
AND
TIME

SEVEN

RITUAL AND COPING

We deal with the pains of passage in a variety of ways. Different persons use different swimming motions to keep themselves afloat above the watery abyss of time and death. But the most general pattern for dealing with mortality seems to be some form of ritual.

The death of Elvis Presley released a tide of random grieving among his devotees, but the strategy of coping was not unlike that connected with the death of Rudolph Valentino years ago. The death was elaborately ritualized in conformity with an established Hollywood design, and millions of mourners found a way of channeling and coping with their grief.

As indicated earlier, ritual may become an end in itself, glossing over the reality of the passage. But even at its worst, ritual does not permit total repression of the pain of passage. At its best, ritual can transform the pain of passage into an enabling and strengthening experience.

It has been helpful for me to think about how our

87

Lord used ritual as a means of fulfilling his messianic mission. His way of dealing with his own passage through time provides guidelines for us, and the assurance of his presence can energize us, not only to cope with passage, but also to make it a source of healing and growth for ourselves and others.

Ritual of closure

I am at that stage of life when I must deal more realistically with my own aging. For the past year I have been devolving my work responsibilities and moving into self-employment and semiretirement. The tasks I am leaving have been most creative for me, and I have never felt more alive and fulfilled than in doing them. I must nevertheless move on. Hence, I am doing for the last time many things that are meaningful for me. It is not as if I shall be doing the same things in another context. I shall not be doing them at all.

Some months ago I served for the last time as director of a training event, the design for which I had helped develop. I was handing over responsibility for the program to a highly qualified successor and close friend, yet I found it very painful to let go. I had shared my feelings with the leadership team for the training event (which included my successor), but as the week progressed, I sensed that something more was needed to bring about closure and to help me lean into the pain of my leaving.

As I mulled over this matter, I came upon an insight that had been hovering on the edge of my consciousness for several months. I found myself identifying with the scene in Acts in which the apostle Paul says good-bye to the elders of Ephesus.

In the middle of the training week, the leadership team was working on a design in relational Bible study. The design involved finding ourselves in the story, identifying with a character, and discovering the good news for us.

In this context I shared Acts 20:17-38, identifying with the leave-taking apostle and trying to be honest about my feelings. As I got into the text, I found myself using Paul's farewell to ritualize my own experience and to process my feelings. In saying good-bye to a ministry and to a group of people most meaningful to me, the words of Paul, as Luke records them, came alive for me:

> I reckon my own life to be worth nothing to me; I only want to complete my mission and finish the work that the Lord Jesus gave me to do, which is to declare the Good News about the grace of God. I have gone about among all of you, preaching the Kingdom of God. And now I know that none of you will ever see me again (Acts 20:24-25 TEV).

I omitted the fairly long exhortation, with which I could not identify, and then read the concluding words:

> When Paul finished, he knelt down with them and prayed. They were all crying as they hugged and kissed him good-bye. They were especially sad because he had said that they would never see him again. And so they went with him to the ship (vv. 36-38).

I looked around the circle of people who had shared with me in a relational ministry of the gospel during the past six years: Marie, Betty Ann, Elsie, Jim, Al. We had been elders together, not in terms of years but in terms of the responsibilities of witness. I was glad I could share my pain of passage with them.

As we talked and shared our feelings and then began to pray together in a tight circle, and then to weep and hold one another, the harsh pain began to lessen and some gladness broke through like the sun shining intermittently through April clouds. The grief was still there, but it had been challenged and changed in some way. It was as if by living into Paul's rite and making it our own, we had begun to experience both dying and resurrection. And we understood the rightness of the concluding sentence in the passage, "And so *they went with him* to the ship." Effective ritual requires the loving *presence* of community, the quality of "withness," which is the essence of the body of Christ.

Jesus' use of ritual

In reflecting further on Paul's ritual closure of his Ephesian ministry (and his premonition seems to have been right, for he never returned), I began to see that this closure was in some sense a replay of the closure in the Upper Room. Jesus' farewell discourses to his disciples hinted at in the synoptics and fully developed in John's gospel are mirrored in Paul's words to the Ephesian elders. So is the substance of Jesus' words to his disciples, "In a little while you will not see me any more" (John 16:16 TEV). Paul says to the elders, "I know that none of you will ever see me again."

I then began to ask how Jesus dealt with other passages in his life, and I became aware that he was highly conscious of ritual. In fulfilling his messianic mission, he used the traditions, ceremonies, festivals, and prophecies of the past, both to identify himself with his people and with all of us and to give meaning to his unique mission.

Thomas Mann's essay on Freud published in 1936 has helped me to understand how Jesus stepped into the robes prepared for him by centuries of visions and prophecies. Mann writes:

> The Ego of antiquity and its consciousness of itself was different from our own, less exclusive, less sharply defined. It was, as it were, open to the back; it received much from the past and by repeating it gave it presentness again. The Spanish scholar Ortega y Gasset puts it that the man of antiquity, before he did anything, took a step backwards, like the bullfighter who leaps back to deliver a mortal thrust. He searched the past for a pattern into which he might slip as into a diving bell, and being thus at once disguised and protected might rush upon his present problem.
>
> We have only to think of Jesus and his life, which was lived in order that that which was written might be fulfilled . . .
>
> (Jesus') words on the cross, about the ninth hour, "Eli, Eli, lama sabachthani?" was not in the least an outburst of despair and disillusionment; but on the contrary, of a lofty Messianic sense of self. For the phrase is not original, not a spontaneous outcry. It stands at the beginning of the Twenty-second Psalm, which from one

> end to the other is an announcement of the
> Messiah. Jesus was quoting and the quotation
> meant: "Yes, it is I."

I am not prepared to agree with Mann that the cry of Jesus "was not in the least an outburst of despair and disillusionment," for I believe that, in a sense, that is exactly what it was. But I do agree that, in uttering it, Jesus was identifying with his role as Messiah.

This says to me that, throughout his life and particularly in his public ministry, Jesus donned the messianic garments that had been woven for him through thousands of years of Hebrew history. In the sad, violent, and beautiful chronicles of Adam, Abraham, Joseph, and David; in Exodus, Kingdom, and Exile; in priest and prophet; in temple and synagogue Jesus saw himself and his mission. The evangelists undoubtedly made additional connections between the Scriptures and the Lord, but the initial identification was his.

The messianic role

We need to ask what the role of the Messiah meant for Jesus. How did he see himself as the Messiah, the anointed king? What was the nature of the deliverance he was committed to bring? And how was his role of king, deliverer, and healer, however conceived, related to his humanity and personhood?

I cannot do justice to a fraction of the theological scholarship devoted to Jesus as Messiah, but I would like to bear witness to two unshakable convictions about Jesus. The first is that he, and not just his followers, saw himself called by his Father to the messianic task and hence devoted his short life to fulfilling that mission. Like an arrow he flew straight for the target. The second conviction is that the substance of his role as Messiah was to be *Immanuel* ("God is with us"). It was Jesus' mission to come and to be with us in our humanity, in its glory and grubbiness; to be so identified with us that not only did he "bear our griefs and carry our sorrows," but he "became a curse for us." He so entered into our human twistedness that he bore its stigma and even its penalty without himself being guilty of it. And he did this to bless, heal, and restore us to a free and joyous relationship with God.

These are awesome words, too deep to clarify, and so often spoken that they may appear unreal and (like a bad funeral sermon) even glossy. But I can testify to what they mean to me as a person. They mean that there is no part of me, no feeling or action of mine to which Jesus is not present. Nothing in me lies outside of his grace and acceptance. Alleluia!

EIGHT

JESUS
AND
PASSAGE

In stressing the humanity of Jesus as his way of identifying with us, we are not diminishing his uniqueness as the Son of God. He was the Son of Man, not only in the special sense that term had in the first century, but in the sense that he was the firstborn of many sisters and brothers; he was one of the human family. But he was also the Son of God, who chose his humanity as a way of fulfilling his divine sonship.

We envisage a dialog within God, the issue of which is that the Son decides to enter the human scene as a human being in order "to bring many sons to glory." This dialog is implied in Philippians 2, in 2 Corinthians 8:9, and perhaps in Romans 8:32. It is present as an assumption in Hebrews. With great theological delicacy it is worked out in Anselm's *Cur Deus Homo?* which asks the question of Christ's *kenosis*, his emptying, literally, why God man?

We need to allow Christ to have the humanity he claims, to believe that his messiahship is worked

94

out in his total identification with us. We need to set aside our reservations about his humanity and our inclination to paint in halos wherever he appears. We need to give him back his human body, his human feelings, his human mind, and to let him be with us as he was with his first followers. We need not take away his power or his intimate relationship to his Father, or the messianic purpose that must have burned in his bones, but we need to purge our minds of the illusion that because he was who he was, things were easy for him, the illusion that keeps whispering to us, "Well, of course, why shouldn't he, considering who he was?"

He brought us the gift of his human presence, and although we sense the design in his visitation, we need to be aware of the coarse fabric of his life. The birth stories in Matthew and Luke (the only references in the New Testament to those events) carry a heavy freight of mystery. They were written down long after the happenings they portray, and the power and glory of the resurrection cast an intense light on them.

The wonder is that, despite such illumination, the truth emerges like a granite outcropping. It must have been like that—a child born of obscure parents in an obscure place, and born like us, "inter faeces et urinam" (between the ordures), as Augustine phrases it. A child with all the defenselessness of infancy and the need for constant care. A child who wailed and dirtied his swaddling and developed sudden and mysterious ailments and struggled, like all

of us, to become a person in the midst of the currents
and crosscurrents of family life.

Jesus and rites

From the beginning, as if to indicate that in this
matter also he was one with the human family, Jesus
participated in the rites of passage and of season.
Luke, who is particularly careful to stress the humanity even of the infant Jesus, tells us that Jesus
was circumcised, like all Jewish babies, when he was
eight days old.

After 40 days, according to the evangelist, Joseph
and Mary went to the Temple in Jerusalem for
Mary's purification, in accordance with Jewish law
(Lev. 12:2-6). At this time also Jesus was *presented*
in the Temple. As a firstborn son, Jesus was required
to be *redeemed* in conformity with an ancient usage
reflected in Exodus 13:13. But Luke either does not
know this requirement or chooses to ignore it as
irrelevant to his purpose. He makes the redemptive
or ransoming ceremony into a dedication, which may
mirror the special dedication of Samuel to the Lord
(1 Sam. 1:24-28).[1]

At the age of 12, according to Luke's account,
Jesus was back in the Temple for the Passover. Luke
shows Jesus as a bright, assertive boy who seems to
be aware of a special relationship to his Father and
is deeply interested in questions of faith. It is amaz-
ing that, in the midst of the beginning of a spate of
legendizing about the childhood of Jesus—a literature reflected in the crude sketches of New Testa-

ment Apocrypha—Luke remains so balanced in his account of the boy Jesus. The child is presented as "sitting with the Jewish teachers, listening to them and asking questions." This is a different Jesus from the one pictured by Hoffman. There Jesus, halo and all, is shown teaching and telling the teachers.

Luke's comment "All who heard him were amazed at his intelligent answers" should probably not be interpreted to mean anything more than what it says. It was an especially moving Bar Mitzvah observance, not a superhuman appearance or theophany. Luke is careful to point out that the boy returns with his parents to his home town and remains obedient to them in the best Jewish tradition.

From that time until he emerged at the age of 30, we know nothing about the life of Jesus.[2] The assumption is that he learned carpentry at his father's workbench. The references are extremely thin. In telling the story of Jesus' appearance in the Nazareth synagogue, Matthew reports that the crowd asked, "Isn't he (Jesus) the carpenter's son?" (Matt. 13:55 TEV). Mark tells the same story but has the people say, "Isn't he the carpenter, the son of Mary?" (Mark 6:3 TEV). Luke omits any reference to carpentry. He says of the synagogue congregation, "They said, 'Isn't he the son of Joseph?'" (Luke 4:22 TEV).

Beyond this, everything is a guess. The highly questionable stories in the New Testament Apocrypha give us little help. An old argument that says Jesus was trained in the Essenic community was revived after the discovery of the Dead Sea scrolls, but it presents more problems than it solves. Rosicrucians have speculated that during the so-called silent years Jesus was trained in the wisdom of the East, but this has no credibility.

All that can be said of these conjectures is that the utterances of Jesus, as recorded in the gospels, show no trace of any esoteric doctrines or disciplines. It is hence safer to assume that Jesus prepared himself for his mission by entering fully into the life of his home community, by making conventional contacts with the religious festivals in Jerusalem, and by pondering deeply the Scriptures that were available to him.

The emergence of Jesus

The passages of birth and puberty are less richly documented than we would like, but Jesus' entrance into the adult world interests all four evangelists. They report the emergence of Jesus in connection with the preaching ministry of John the Baptist. John's proclamation about the coming of the kingdom has created a large and ambivalent hearing among the Jewish people.

That John and his mission are important to Jesus we can conclude from John's baptism of Jesus and John's part in several conversations between Jesus and his disciples. But the gospels suggest an even closer connection. John is seen as the forerunner of Jesus, the announcer of his coming and his mission.

So important, in fact, is the Baptist in the ministry of our Lord that biblical scholars have suggested that some of the followers of John saw Jesus as pre-empting John's ministry. A community of faith growing out of the Baptist's ministry seems to have lasted several centuries. Acts tells us that the Alexandrian teacher Apollos "knew only the baptism of John" (18:25 TEV), even though "he had been instructed in the Way of the Lord, and with great enthusiasm he proclaimed and taught correctly the facts about Jesus." This suggests that in certain Christian circles the Baptist and his ministry were actively remembered.

Whatever the facts about a John the Baptist cult, the gospels do not present Jesus and John in competition, nor is Jesus' emergence seen as motivated by rivalry. Rather, Jesus and John appear to have had a previous relationship of mutual respect and support in which both were ready to recognize the merit of the other's ministry. This relationship is acknowledged in the baptism. But the baptism also helps define John's relationship to Jesus. John sees himself as the one who "prepares the way" for Jesus. Hence Jesus is "greater" than he.[3]

All four gospels use Isaiah's words to introduce the Baptist: "A voice cries out, 'Prepare in the wilderness a road for the Lord! Clear the way in the desert for our God!'" (Isa. 40:3 TEV). This unanimity is important, for it means that all four evangelists see the ministry of Jesus as the messianic drama for which John is the preparer and herald.

There are differences among the evangelists' writings, but there are also striking similarities. All the gospels except John's tell of Jesus' baptism at the

99

hand of the Baptist. All contrast John's water baptism with that of Jesus, which is by the Holy Spirit. All refer to John's self-confessed unworthiness to wear the shoes or untie the shoelaces of Jesus. Two of the four report questions about John's identity. Is he Christ, or Elijah returned to life, or a prophet?

The significance of Jesus' baptism

Jesus celebrates his entrance on his public ministry by submitting to the baptism of John. Baptism is a significant passage in his life and a highly meaningful ritual for him. It is also a symbolic act pointing forward to his death and burial as integral to his messianic mission. Hence his words in response to John's protest that he, the Baptist, ought indeed to be baptized by Jesus: "Let it be so for now. For in this way we shall do all that God requires" (Matt. 3:15 TEV).[4]

In all four gospels the Holy Spirit is seen descending like a dove on Jesus. In the first three gospels the revelation of the Spirit is combined with a voice from heaven that validates Jesus as the Son of God. In John's gospel the baptism of Jesus by John the Baptist is not directly mentioned, and although the Spirit comes in the form of a dove, the meaning is somewhat different.

Here, as elsewhere in the gospel of John, a *finished* or almost finished Christ is presented. It is as if John were looking at the life of Jesus almost entirely from the other side of the resurrection. Rather

100

than seeing Jesus as struggling to complete the messianic mission, John sees him as trying to have his lordship accepted. The earthly ministry of Jesus, in John's gospel, is a revelation of the glory. "The Word became a human being and, full of grace and truth, lived among us. We saw his glory, the glory which he received as the Father's only Son" (John 1:14 TEV).[5]

In John, for example, there is no reference to a wilderness temptation and only a faint echo of the struggle in Gethsemane.[6] In John's record the baptism of Jesus by the Baptist (which in the synoptic gospels is an entry into the struggles inherent in the messianic mission) is probably omitted or only implicitly stated because John is intent on showing that the Baptist saw Jesus as the already glorified Savior. John the Baptist's testimony at the baptismal site, "Behold, the Lamb of God, who takes away the sin of the world!" comes so early in the career of Jesus as to be prophetic vision rather than accomplished fact. But it says what John's gospel intends to say, namely, that the struggle is over and that now the revealed Son of God needs only to be accepted and witnessed to.

The baptism at the hands of John represents another passage for Jesus. After his years of preparation, he gives up his close association with his hometown and his relationship to the Baptist, about which we know almost nothing. Luke reports the kinship of John and Jesus, but nothing further is said about this in any of the gospels. John's bittersweet attitude suggests how difficult it was for him to step

101

aside in favor of Jesus. His feelings are suggested in a passage in John's gospel in which the alarm of John's disciples and the reconciling attitude of the Baptist are both reflected:

> Some of John's disciples began arguing with a Jew about the matter of ritual washing. So they went to John and told him, "Teacher, you remember the man who was with you on the east side of the Jordan, the one you spoke about? Well, he is baptizing now, and everyone is going to him!"
>
> John answered, "No one can have anything unless God gives it to him. You yourselves are my witnesses that I said, 'I am not the Messiah, but I have been sent ahead of him.' The bridegroom is the one to whom the bride belongs; but the bridegroom's friend, who stands by and listens, is glad when he hears the bridegroom's voice. This is how my own happiness is made complete. He must become more important while I become less important" (John 3:25-30 TEV).

Jesus tested

The outline of the messianic scenario that emerges so clearly in Jesus' submission to the baptism of John also appears in the temptation account immediately following. The wilderness scene, intrinsic to biblical stories of testing and preparation, the symbolic 40 days of fasting and prayer, the triple encounter with the Adversary, the use of Scriptures as weapon and counterweapon (by false and true prophets)—all this is ritual recurrence. Place, characters, and script have been long in the making.

If it is true that Jesus assumes that messianic robe prepared for him by biblical history and prophecy, it should be possible to find clues in the Old Testament to the meaning of the temptation of Jesus. In *Seven Pillars of Wisdom,* Lawrence of Arabia argues that monotheism is born in the desert and polytheism in the more complex setting of urban life. There may be some truth in his contention, but in the Old Testament the desert setting provides more than a revelation of the one God. The desert seems always to be the place in which a lone man without any prop is pitted against God or is confronted by a divine vocation or mission. The scene is pure—not theologically simple, but reducing the elements of the drama to clear confrontation. Jacob wrestles with God at Jabbok (Peniel) ; Moses meets God at the burning bush; Israel and Yahweh struggle 40 years on the wilderness stage; Elijah trudges for 40 days to Horeb, the mount of God; Job talks with the Almighty in a life rendered naked by calamity.

Those who take part in these desert encounters seem to develop a clearer sense of personal identity (Who am I? Who is God?), a better understanding of how that identity (or name) is related to their calling (I am called to this but not to that), and a deeper trust in God's love (God promises not to forsake me, but to be with me in doing what I have been asked to do).

Jesus enters into the wilderness in touch with his past. In confronting the grim Adversary, he was absolutely alone, but he carried with him the memory and the promise of those who had gone before. God was with him, but so were Jacob, Moses, Elijah, Job, and the Baptist. Hence, in going into the desert alone, he might appropriately have used the words he spoke at his baptism: "We do well to conform in this way with all that God requires" (Matt. 3:15 NEB).

The Jesus who appears at the Jordan to be baptized by John, who is led by the Spirit into the wilderness and there encounters the "dread spirit, the spirit of self-destruction and non-existence" (Dostoevsky) seems amazingly strong and self-possessed. We detect no chinks in his armor, no fumbling starts, none of the sweaty uncertainty we associate with beginning a new job. How can we put together this "cool" with the humanity of Jesus? I believe that the "presence" of Jesus on these occasions, what his chroniclers report as "authority," is related to his messianic mission. The power in what he says and in what he does flows from what he claims to be.

But what he claims to be cannot be separated from what he is. His messianic calling is to be "Immanuel" (God with us), that is, to be God in human form, emptied of his glory (Philippians 2) and sharing in our weakness and vulnerability. This must include both uncertainty and self-doubting. How else can we account for the intensity of his prayer life and for the flashes of feeling that are everywhere present?

Jesus thus lives and acts as the Messiah, but in actualizing the messianic role, he writes a new script —a human spirit. And when he dies, he dies a naked criminal, seemingly stripped of the messianic robes he wore so authentically, and yet, in his stripping and emptying, more Messiah than ever.

The ambivalence of Jesus

The classical discussions of the humanity of Jesus have usually centered around his physical vulnerability: his hunger and thirst, his weariness, his weakness, the maceration of his passion. But much more striking to me is his ambivalence about his calling, the interior struggle, not so much with his fitness to do what is asked of him as with his willingness to do it. I see this in his irritation when confronting Jewish leaders, and in his frustration with his disciples. But I see it particularly when a temptation moves into sharp focus, as in the wilderness encounter with the devil, his confrontation with Peter at Caesarea Philippi, and his final bout in the Garden.

The vigor with which he thrusts away these temptations suggests that they come close to the target. Many, many times as a gifted teacher and prophet he must have asked himself if the way that was charted for him was not a final madness. His association with insensitive people, his unending contact with the physically and emotionally needy, his controversial encounters with the religious leaders of his day, many of whom must have been admirable people who under different circumstances might have been his friends—what did it all mean?

When Jesus began his public ministry, he must have felt all these stresses and ambiguities. He clearly understood the thrust if not the details of his mission, but as the human person he was, he must have been repelled by its threat of hostility, misunderstanding, conflict, and pain.

And what about his deliberate rejection of marriage and family? Did not this add to the strangeness and unreality of his mission? The texts do not conceal his comfortable relationship to women or his fondness for children; he has none of John the Baptist's asceticism. Yet he chooses to be alone in this way—perhaps unencumbered, but unsustained as well.

The complexity of Jesus

The Jesus the gospels give us is thus a richly complex person. He communicates the conviction and authority of a man who knows what he is about, but he treads constantly the volcanic ground of temptation and risk. Despite this ambivalence, traditional Christian theology has worked with the assumption that from the beginning Jesus was fully aware and accepting of his destiny and his mission. In its understandable desire to preserve the glory of the exalted Christ, this theology has tended to deprive the earthly life of Jesus of its more human dimension and to make him, in the days of his flesh, all-knowing and all-powerful, if not everywhere present.

Such a heavy freight of divinity has given Jesus' life on earth a certain woodenness. It has removed from him much of the anxiety about the future that was surely his, and it has freed his turbulent life of the agony of choice. From this perspective the wilderness temptations look like programmed events in a script of which he had detailed awareness from the outset.

I say this not to make Jesus merely human or to divest him of those functions of his messiahship that he himself assumed. I believe with the earthly witnesses that Jesus was aware of the scope as well as the hazards of his mission when he embarked on it. He knew what he was called on to do. But he seems not to have known this in detail. The mission was not an accomplished fact until it was accomplished, and the glory and terror of Jesus' mission lay in the possibility of it failing or in his failing it. Only the risk, the choice, the doubtful issue of the struggle could give him a true victory or the Father a victory in him.

This knowing and not knowing is the ground for Paul's richly ambiguous statement about Jesus in the introductory paragraph of Romans:

> This gospel . . . is about his Son: on the human level he was born of David's stock, but on the level of the spirit—the Holy Spirit—he was declared Son of God by a mighty act in that he rose from the dead: it is about Jesus Christ our Lord (Rom. 1:2-4 NEB).

Ambiguity is also present in Paul's moving description of the *kenosis* ("emptying") of Jesus in Philippians.

> Let your bearing towards one another arise out of your life in Christ Jesus. For the divine nature was his from the first; yet he did not think to snatch at equality with God, but made himself nothing, assuming the nature of a slave. Bearing the human likeness, revealed in human

107

shape, he humbled himself, and in obedience accepted even death—death on a cross. Therefore God raised him to the heights and bestowed on him the name above all names, that at the name of Jesus every knee should bow—in heaven, on earth, and in the depths—and every tongue confess, "Jesus Christ is Lord," to the glory of God the Father (Phil. 2:5-11 NEB).

Both of these passages suggest the genuine humanity of Jesus and thus the reality of his struggle. But they also suggest — Philippians much more clearly—that the "emptying" of Jesus, his becoming human, was a prior choice. He chose to become like us, and having chosen that, he chose to enter the full implications of his messiahship.

Those implications must have been suspected by him but not fully known. Indeed, they could not be known until they had been carried out. We have said that Jesus assumed the robes of his messiahship. It is perhaps more accurate to say that, as he proceeded with his mission, he put together or had put together for him an even richer messianic robe than the Old Testament had prepared for him. And the most striking thread in the fabric of that robe was blood—the red thread of his humanity, which remained authentic until the end.

The declaration of his mission

One of the most vivid messianic scenes from the early ministry of our Lord is his first visit to Nazareth after his baptism, as Luke records it.[7] Luke writes that Jesus went to the synagogue on the Sab-

108

bath day, "as his custom was." There he read Isaiah 61:1-2 and proclaimed that *that* Scripture was now fulfilled.

According to Luke, the townspeople of Nazareth could accept the proclamation of the year of the Lord, but not the judgment of Jesus that they were unready to hear him. They responded angrily, and in rejecting him they actually fulfilled the prophecy he had uttered about them. (In this part of the messianic scenario, which has to do with the "rejected prophet," Jesus alludes not only to Isaiah but to Elijah and Elisha.)

The rejection by his own in Nazareth becomes a foreshadowing of the treatment Jesus was to receive at the hands of most of his people. Matthew and Mark, both drawing on the same source, say about the people of Nazareth, "and so they rejected him" (TEV). John, speaking more generally, writes, "he came to his own country, but his own people did not receive him" (John 1:11 TEV).

The theme of the unheeded prophet or the suffering servant who is "despised and rejected" is thus restated. It has been introduced earlier in the prophecy of Simeon. Jesus, says Simeon, has been chosen by God "for the destruction and the salvation of many in Israel. He will be a sign from God which many people will speak against and so reveal their secret thoughts" (Luke 2:34-35 TEV).

Mark tells us that on the occasion in Nazareth Jesus was "greatly surprised" because his townspeople "did not have faith" (Mark 6:6 TEV). The composite picture suggests a Jesus who, on the one

109

hand, discerns that in his messianic role he can expect rejection by his people (ultimately by most of them) and who, on the other, registers amazement that they will not hear him.

The messianic robe

Every episode adds bright and dark colors to the messianic robe. The design for that robe is provided by the past but also enlarged and enriched by the present. The Sermon on the Mount; maxim and parable; the calling and training of the twelve; miracles of healing, freeing, and raising; the feeding of thousands; encounters with individuals; confrontations with the religious and political establishments; the transfiguration; the cleansing of the Temple; the triumphal entry; the Passover meal in the Upper Room; and even the crucifixion—all are partly remembered and entered into as parts of the divine scenario and partly new and shocking, like touching a bare wire.

Jesus as the lawgiver speaks like Moses from the mountain. The 12 disciples are to inherit the 12 thrones of Israel. The miracles of Elijah and Elisha are mirrored in Jesus' healing work. The manna in the wilderness is remembered in feeding the multitudes. Jesus' collision with religious and political power systems reminds us of prophets such as Moses, Samuel, Nathan, Elijah, Amos, Isaiah, Micah, and Jeremiah. In the transfiguration, Old Testament law and prophecy are present in the persons of Moses and Elijah. The triumphal entry is filled with parallels and analogues from the Old Testament (Ps. 118:26, Hab. 2:11, Jer. 6:6, Ezek. 4:2, Isa. 29:6 and 62:11, Zech. 9:9, 2 Kings 9:13). In the cleansing of the Temple, ancient words of Jeremiah, Isaiah, and Malachi are heard again.[8]

The Passion drama is too well known to need detailed commentary. It is obvious from the texts that Jesus in the midst of it, as well as his followers and the evangelists in remembering it, identifies himself with prophetic expectations. Two of the great constituting events for the people of God in the Old Testament are the Passover and the miracle of the Sea. They are present in the messianic scenario of Jesus. At the end he not only celebrates the Passover with his disciples; he is the lamb led to the slaughter, the pascal lamb. His death becomes a restatement of the primal baptism of the Red Sea, his resurrection a triumphant recapitulation of the deliverance.

But although the scenario has already been suggested in what has gone before, the action of Jesus is in no way automatic. Choice is present to the end. Jesus, with unbelievable dignity and knowing that his hour has come, chooses to give up the last vestige of his power and to accept the indignity of the Passion. The death that has been present at the beginning, has hovered like a shadow during the silent years, and has grown into ominous dusk during his few months of ministry, is now almost solid darkness. The insult of the trials, the appearance before Pilate, the dreary comedy with the soldiers in the Praetorium, the procession to the cross, the nail-

111

ing fast, the reviling, the failure of strength, the final vulnerability are summed up in the cry of dereliction, *Eloi, Eloi, lama sabachthani,* the Aramaic rendering of words from Psalm 22, "My God, my God, why have you abandoned me?" (TEV).

This is truly the way of sorrows, and yet, as Thomas Mann points out, the horror is confronted within the framework of the messianic mission. Jesus dies "as it was foretold." The abandonment is real, but it is not capricious or meaningless.

Thus ends the dolorous side of the messianic scenario. Sustained by his central role in the salvation drama, by his intimate communion with his Father, the presence of angels, and the brittle support of his followers, Jesus remains steadfast to the end. We need hardly wonder that the impression he left on those who were to chronicle his ministry and particularly his death was one of integrity and authenticity. He not only spoke, he lived and died with authority.

NINE

THE VULNERABLE JESUS

The messianic mission anticipated in the Scriptures is the leitmotif, the dominant theme of the drama, but there is another side. The credibility of the gospel accounts rests upon their willingness to let this other side be implied and even stated.

I have spoken of the human, vulnerable, even self-doubting side of our Lord as though it stood over against the calmer, more assured, and mission-oriented side. This may suggest a double character. Such there certainly was, but it was not schizophrenic or destructive in any way. It was contrapuntal and creatively ambivalent. The vulnerable Jesus was, in fact, indispensable for the actualization of the messiahship.

In the early years of the church, when Greek theologians got hold of this ambivalence, they were drawn into centuries of dialectical struggle. In which way was Christ both God and man? Did he have one nature or two, one will or two?

There is no way that these questions can be fully answered. I suggest the struggle only to indicate

113

that the closer we push to the Jesus of the gospels, the more we become aware of the doubleness of his dynamic nature.

And indeed it had to be so, not by the necessities of nature, but by the imperatives of grace. A less human Jesus could not have identified with us, nor could we have identified with him. The writer of the epistle to the Hebrews makes Christ's priestly function for us dependent on his vulnerability: "For ours is not a high priest unable to sympathize with our weaknesses, but one who, because of his likeness to us, has been tested every way, only without sin" (Heb. 4:15 NEB).

The availability of Jesus to me rests on his vulnerability. In his brief life and extremely brief ministry, he passed through the transitions that are common to all of us and felt the pain of passage with us. The hesitancy, self-doubting, and anxiety we perceive in him are the burdens of his incarnation, his *kenosis,* and the brittleness we sense in him in the face of them makes him an effective priest for us.

Jesus' inner struggle

The fragmentary accounts we have of the infancy and boyhood of Jesus make us aware of the shadows gathering around him and of his consciousness of a calling, but they do not help us get inside him. The inner struggle is first indicated in the temptation stories that follow upon his baptism.

Jesus' encounter with the devil comes immediately

114

after the Holy Spirit has descended on him in the form of a dove. This suggests that the temptations are related to an activation of Jesus' unique gifts and powers. At that moment he must have sensed the exhilaration of his calling and the wealth of his endowments. He must have been aware of these earlier, since he could not have leaped fully armed into his task, but then they had been matters of fantasy, and the messianic scenario of which he must have had some consciousness counseled him to wait.

Now he has experienced the robing, and he is ready. The Spirit who had validated him and his ministry leads him into the wilderness to be tested. In the Lord's Prayer we are asked to plead that we not be led into temptation, yet this was precisely Jesus' experience.

What were these temptations? Myron Madden speaks of the wilderness experience as a "tearing up of the blueprints" for Jesus. This sounds plausible. We are not tempted with things that are not intensely desirable, and we can trace in each of the temptations the precise routes that Jesus may have wanted to take to serve God and his people. That he did not take these routes indicates his profound consciousness of what the messianic mission was, but his thinking about them presents him to us as vulnerable.

Some years ago I read through hundreds of applications written by high school seniors as part of their effort to get into college. The final blank in the application asked students to state their motivation for wanting a university education. A startling number of the applicants indicated that their motive was to serve—truth, humanity, world peace, minorities, etc. I am sure that most of these statements were sincere. I am equally sure that few of the applicants had faced the question of how these goals were to be attained and at what cost.

These must have been Jesus' questions before and during the testing. His temptation was not to abandon his ultimate goals but to waver before the choice of how to reach them and the price that would be expected of him.

Using his power to feed himself and others, using his power to protect himself and render himself invulnerable, allying himself with the glory and power available in the world—these things would have had two effects. They would have isolated him from the God on whose power he depended, and they would have separated him from the people he came to serve.

In his adult life, Jesus' separation from his past in baptism brought the first pain of passage. The second came with the decision to be rid of self-deception and to maintain his living contact with God and with people. The pain of this passage must have been unbelievable for a person as gifted and charismatic as Jesus. He was physically hungry and thirsty from his wilderness sojourn, but his rejection of a life filled with green valleys and fair gardens must have filled him with the burning thirst and hunger of that inner wilderness which is reality and integrity. It is no accident that a few months later he was to die thirsty. Matthew tells us that when

116

his wilderness trial was over, angels ministered to him. Let us hope that they came often.

Getting started

After clarifying ends and means, the second step on the career ladder is to find acceptance and support for what we are about. Jesus' appearance in the Nazareth synagogue begins on a note of acceptance and approval. It seems for a moment as if his old friends are going to give him the keys to the city. If Jesus was like us, such approval must have been momentarily attractive to him, if not seductive. It was a form of the temptation he had already toyed with in the wilderness—the dominion and glory of kingdoms.

His vulnerability appears in the vehemence with which he replies to their question, "Is not this the carpenter's son?" A professor once told my class that Jesus never fled from his enemies, but he often fled from his friends. His enemies helped to define his person and his mission; his friends muddied them. Some of that awareness must have been present in his antagonistic words to the people of Nazareth. He would not be trapped in the coziness of their favor.

In any event, it was a passage. In it Jesus must have said good-bye to some of the people who had believed in him and helped him get under way. They may have hoped that he would bring fame to their town and satisfaction to them. They were cruelly disappointed. He would not limit himself to their paro-

117

chial interests. He was hearing "a different drummer." And they were infuriated.

The episode was a paradigm or model of his relationship to his people as a whole. At one level, I am sure, Jesus wanted the favor of his people as much as anything. He was not a misanthrope. He wanted to be a son of duty, receiving the love, admiration, and respect of his fellows. He did not return to Nazareth to irritate and goad his friends. He came to offer a gift. But the gift had to be received on the terms under which it was offered. The unwillingness of his people to accept the terms led to rupture.

Up and down the ladder

Jesus must have been aware of his growing acceptance by the people. It was a burden, and he often fled from it in order to survive. But it was also an inspiration. Someone has said that the temptations Jesus faced in the wilderness were present with him every day of his ministry. That is certainly true. The growing crowds, the rapt attention, the enthusiastic response to his teaching and to his acts of power, the development of an inner circle of attractive and supportive men and women, the increasing numbers of scholarly and politically influential people who mingled with the crowds—what popular preacher would fail to be pleased by such a response? It did not cause our Lord to veer from his messianic purpose, but it must have forced him to deal with it.

Hence his querying of the disciples, as recorded

118

in Matthew 16:13-20, should probably not be seen as merely an occasion for having his messianic role stated. There is in the question "Who do men say that the Son of Man is?" also the poignancy of ordinary life at midchannel: What is the impression people have of me? Am I getting across? What are they expecting of me?

John records an episode not in the other gospels, but not unlike the passage in Matthew. The crowds, after being fed by the miracle of bread, try to take Jesus "to make him king by force" (John 6:15 TEV).

Personal popularity always expresses itself in idolization, and Jesus could not have been unaware that his successes had made him adored by thousands of people. In their efforts to give him his due, they speak of him as John the Baptist, Elijah, Jeremiah, or one of the other prophets. There is a powerful attraction in being thought a god, especially one who does not have to die.

Caught in the toils of the temptation, Jesus pushes for a clearer understanding of his role. It is then that Peter gives his historic witness, "You are the Messiah, the Son of the living God." To be a god or a revivified prophet is one thing; to be the Messiah is something else. Jesus' response to Peter seems in part motivated by his gratitude for having his role defined by him. It must have been a relief to be truly understood by someone. He plays on Simon Peter's name and calls him the rock on which he will build the church.

But it becomes clear almost immediately that

119

Peter has not understood what the messianic role meant, for when Jesus talks about his imminent sufferings in Jerusalem, Peter takes him aside and begins to rebuke him. "God forbid it, Lord!" he said. "That must never happen to you!" Jesus' response is very intense: "Get away from me, Satan! You are an obstacle in my way, because these thoughts of yours don't come from God, but from man" (Matt. 16:22-24 TEV).

Jesus is probably saying that Peter has stated Jesus' feelings exactly. The feelings are not only those of the impulsive disciple, but those of the Lord himself. Hence the vehemence. In Peter's words Jesus hears the wilderness words repeated. The messianic role is not to die but to conquer—that is the devil's reasoning.

Keys to Jesus' humanity

We should attend to those places in the life and ministry of Jesus where we sense his acute discouragement, impatience, and anger surfacing. These places, marvelously preserved by faithful witnesses, are keys to his humanity and vulnerability. His religious and political opponents, his followers, his disciples, and even his own family bring out the disillusionment and anger in him.

We are reminded of Thomas More's irritation with his wife in *A Man for All Seasons*. Anger is not what we have been led to expect from saints. We assume they have laid aside their humanity in order to be saints. Of course, the opposite is true.

No one is so human as the saints. Their awareness of their humanity makes them saints.

Jesus' ire before his religious and political opponents seems rooted in his conviction that they are out to get him—a reasonable inference. Hence the anger probably stems from fear as well as from indignation and contempt. His classic words about Herod are an index to such feelings: "Go and tell that fox!"

With his followers and his family, Jesus' anger is based on impatience, frustration, and discouragement. He does not see them as wicked or even stupid, but as fearful and slow to believe and hence not supportive of his mission.

But whatever the source of Jesus' feelings, they emerge from his humanity and particularly from his uncertainty that he can get the job done. It is the acceptance of the full burden of his humanity that makes his praying so significant. He is fighting for his life. The desperate prayer in the Garden is hence only a consummation of a succession of such encounters.

Jesus spent the last few months of his life and ministry in Judea. Hostility had certainly been present in Galilee, but its ultimate concentration was in Judea and particularly Jerusalem. Jesus knew that the final clash between him and the authorities would come there.

The final months manifest extremes of wild enthusiasm toward Jesus on the one hand and, on the other, increasing peevishness, disinterest, squabbling, hostility, and rage. John tells us that "many of Jesus' followers turned back and would not go with him any more" (John 6:66 TEV). Matthew records that the disciples raised questions about their reward for following him (Matt. 19:27), an indication of disenchantment. The disciples quarrel frequently about who is the greatest, who is to sit on his right hand and his left, etc. Judas, for whatever motives, begins to plan to betray him.

And Jesus' mood perceptibly darkens. His parables seem more solemn, his teaching more terminal and apocalyptic, his actions more drastic (for example, he curses the fig tree, laments over Jerusalem, and cleanses the temple). He also raises the question whether, on his return, he will find any faith at all.

We detect in all of this Jesus' growing awareness that he is coming to the point of no return. The messianic scenario is carrying him swiftly toward his death, and the options are no longer, as they may once have been, growing support and popularity on the one hand or growing opposition on the other. The moves on the chessboard are now pitifully few.

In all of this, Jesus' reactions are strikingly human. Until the last moment in the Garden, he shows a range of feelings that suggest his inner stress. He now has no hope for a happier earthly destiny, not even an obscure life in his native town, but he wants out of the lethal trap in which he finds himself. He wants the cup to pass. He does not want to die, at least not in this way. The scene in the Garden is thus the final and most dramatic revelation of his humanity and vulnerability.

And then the end will come

After the betrayal of Judas and throughout the farcical process that passes for justice, including the jesting of the guard in the Praetorium, Jesus remains strangely quiet and self-controlled. All the evangelists, including John, testify to Jesus' silence before his accusers. When he speaks at all, it is not in the effort to convince anyone but as if to hasten the end of the drama. In other words, he seems totally identified with the messianic role. This does not mean that he is no longer human, but only that the human and the messianic are now in concert.

Even the words of dereliction on the cross, though the most human and movingly apt of all his words, are at the same time a faithful rendering of the messianic script. Thomas Mann claims that the words are addressed to the messianic expectation and that they mean, "It is I." If that is so, then "It is finished," which only John records as the last utterance of Jesus, means that the last temptation has been overcome, the temptation not to die as the Messiah.

The strength for this—and what unimaginable strength it took!—must have come in part from Jesus' awareness that he was at one level acting out, living out, and dying out the ancient messianic hope. He leaned into his past. As the triumphs as well as the hostilities grew, the actions he performed as well as the words he uttered were drawn in part from the past which he had chosen and which had chosen him. He was fulfillment.

But the messianic action, when it was performed,

123

was never exactly like the prophetic expectation. There was in the fulfillment also the terrifyingly new—the raw and brutal. The drama was ancient and stylized, like a tragedy by Aeschylus, but it was also contemporary and open-ended like the unbridled plays of the late '60s.

Hence the messianic drama could never have been safe and comfortable for Jesus, as some rituals tend to become. To don the armor of the champion meant to invite hostility. Jesus required a constant source of new energy. Such energy, the record tells us, came to him when he prayed.

Jesus prays

How did Jesus pray—liturgically, following the archaic patterns with which he was familiar, or spontaneously?

When I was a child I was exposed to both types. To me they often were (and I am afraid still are) boring.

There is one thing I am absolutely sure of. Jesus did not do things that bored him. He has something to say about vain repetitions, suggesting that prayer for the sake of prayer did not interest him. Hence, he must have prayed in a way that mattered.

What did matter to him? I think two things were preeminent. The first was evidence that he was carrying out his Father's mission or that the Father's work was being done through him. Such evidence must have made him thankful. We glimpse

124

his gratitude: "Father, Lord of heaven and earth! I thank you because you have shown to the unlearned what you have hidden from the wise and learned. Yes, Father, this was how you were pleased to have it happen" (Matt. 11:25-26 TEV).

The second preeminent concern must have been closely related to the first. Jesus wanted help with the next step on the road of obedience. He wanted to finish the work the Father had entrusted to him. That concern is reflected in what we call the Lord's Prayer and in the Gethsemane prayer. Such prayers could never have been routine. Like the prayers of gratitude, they must have been impassioned. The writer of Hebrews, using an unidentified source, tells us that "in his life on earth Jesus made his prayers and requests with loud cries and tears to God who could save him from death. Because he was humble and devoted, God heard him" (Heb. 5:7 TEV).

What was the scene of these desperate prayers? Was it the wilderness, the garden, the cross? We don't know, but we do know that, for our Lord, prayer was violent wrestling with God, accompanied by tears and cries and, in at least one instance, bloody sweat.[1]

Such prayer helped Jesus stay on course. Hebrews tells us that "even though he was God's Son, he learned through his sufferings to be obedient" (Heb. 5:8 TEV). It is difficult to understand what this means unless we see it in the context of his mission and his prayer life. Each step of the scenario that Jesus completed he brought to God in intimate conversation. The revelation of God's will in that step

125

taught him how to be obedient in the next one. His deep dependence on his Father saved him from the arrogance of achievement and from absolute despair about what lay ahead.

The disciples' role

But if Jesus was helped through prayer, as we are persuaded he was, what can we say about the help he must have looked for in his disciples? Traditionally these men have been seen as the vanguard of that large army of apostolic messengers which was to march across the Mediterranean world in the next few centuries. However, the close circle of twelve seems not to have produced—except in elaborately embroidered legends—more than three or four who shared leadership in the apostolic church. At least we have no reliable record of it.

But even if we assume that preaching was the primary mission of the twelve, as well as of the wider circle, we cannot escape the conclusion that Jesus saw his disciples as something more than people in training for a task.

Let us review briefly what the gospels tell us about the disciples. Mark says: "Then Jesus went up a hill and called to himself the men he wanted. They came to him, and he chose twelve, whom he named apostles. 'I have chosen you to be with me,' he told them. 'I will also send you out to preach, and you will have authority to drive out demons' " (Mark 3:13-15 TEV). So he appointed the twelve.

Luke is even less informative. He writes: "When

126

day came, he called his disciples to him and chose twelve of them, whom he named apostles" (Luke 6:13 TEV). Matthew writes: "Jesus called his twelve disciples together and gave them authority to drive out evil spirits and to heal every disease and every sickness" (Matt. 10:1 TEV).

Matthew gives us an account of a "mission" by the twelve, which Mark puts later in the story (6:6-13) and which Luke also includes (9:1-6). But Luke echoes the same instructions in the sending out of the seventy-two.

What are we to conclude from this? That the twelve were to be apostles, witnesses to the coming kingdom and active in the ministries of healing and driving out demons? Certainly. But if we look at the record, this activity seems to have left very little impact. In fact, it is the seventy-two (Luke 10:17-20) and not the twelve who came back triumphant from their mission.[2]

Can we infer from this that the twelve had a mission other than preaching the works of power, which are spelled out so clearly in the gospels? Mark suggests it. He reports Jesus calling to himself the "men he wanted," and saying to them, "I have chosen you to be with me. I will *also* send you out to preach, and you will have authority to drive out demons."

This suggests that one of the primary roles of the disciples was simply to *be with* Jesus, to form an intentional community with him in order to support him in his messianic mission. That the disciples saw

127

it that way is indicated by Peter's words when a successor is to be selected for Judas:

> So then, someone must join us as a witness to the resurrection of the Lord Jesus. He must be one of those who were in our group during the whole time that the Lord Jesus traveled about with us, beginning from the time John preached his message of baptism until the day Jesus was taken up from us into heaven (Acts 1:21-22 TEV).

The emphasis in the passage is clearly upon "a witness to the resurrection," but it is significant that such a witness must be drawn from the group that was with Jesus from the beginning. The importance of the "withness" should not be lost sight of.

Jesus' family of friends

The meaning of "being with" Jesus as a primary mission of the disciples becomes clearer if we put it in the context of Jesus' messiahship. According to Matthew 1:23, Jesus was Immanuel ("God is with us"). The intentional community that Jesus formed by calling the twelve and by adding others must have been seen by him as his family—people he could support and enable and people he hoped would support and enable him.

He was *with* them, but he also wanted them to be *with* him. Because he was human, our Lord felt the need of people with whom he could share his life. In addition to the seventy-two, the gospels speak of the supportive presence of a community of women, some of whom were present with him at

128

the cross,[3] and of the close friendship of the family at Bethany.

Among the many and varied followers who must have surrounded Jesus, the twelve nevertheless had a special place. Within the tight circle, Peter, James, and John seem to have had an even more select status. It was these three who followed him to the house of Jairus, to the mount of transfiguration, and to the place of struggle in the Garden.

What did Jesus hope or expect from his intimate circle? Why did he want the disciples with him? We can conclude from Jesus' statements to his disciples that what he looked for in them was acceptance of his messianic mission and of the coming kingdom and awareness of its signs, and willingness to follow out its implications in witness and in demonstrations of power. The testimony of Simon Peter in Matthew, "You are the Messiah, the Son of the living God," must be seen in the context of these expectations, as must the Johannine echo of these words in John's gospel: "Lord, to whom would we go? You have the words that give eternal life. And now we believe and know that you are the Holy One who has come from God" (John 6:68-69 TEV).

But Jesus seems to have had other expectations of his disciples that they did not fulfill. These related not so much to an intellectual acceptance of Jesus' mission or even to a willingness to help advance it as to an entering into the messianic mission itself. When Jesus talks to the twelve about his imminent suffering and death or takes the three apart with him, we sense his urgent need to be heard at a deeper than intellectual level, to be loved, to be sustained, and to be enabled in the work he is called to do.

This is stated more explicitly in John's gospel than in the synoptics, particularly in the farewell discourses. Jesus says, "I do not call you servants any longer, because a servant does not know what his master is doing. Instead, I call you friends, because I have told you everything I heard from my Father" (John 15:15 TEV).

What this suggests is the desire of Jesus to have the disciples with him in intimate involvement, showing the concern he manifested toward them. In this context he speaks about love, the love of his Father for him, his love for them, and their love for one another.

The desire for close friendship is also expressed in the synoptics. In Luke 22:15 (TEV), Jesus says to the twelve at the Last Supper, "I have wanted so much to eat this Passover meal *with you* before I suffer!"

The disciples' failures

But the twelve consistently disappoint him. He spends a great deal of time rebuking them for their small faith, for their lack of perception of what he is doing, even for their actual blocking of his ministry. He also seems troubled by their unwillingness to see that he also has needs. In this respect the women who accompany Jesus seem more sensitive.

The disciples need to make Jesus a parent figure, responsible for their safety, comfort, and discipline,

130

and for their future reward. They seldom see themselves as adults (friends) who are called upon to
be vulnerably human and hence able to identify with
and support Jesus. Perhaps that is why John records
this saying of Jesus: "But I am telling you the truth:
it is better for you that I go away, because if I do
not go, the Helper will not come to you" (John 16:7
TEV).

That Jesus looked for more from his disciples than
he found is evident from the Gethsemane story.

> Then Jesus went with his disciples to a place
> called Gethsemane, and he said to them, "Sit
> here while I go over there and pray." He took
> with him Peter and the two sons of Zebedee.
> Grief and anguish came over him, and he said to
> them, *"The sorrow in my heart is so great that
> it almost crushes me. Stay here and keep watch
> with me."*
>
> He went a little farther on, threw himself
> downward on the ground, and prayed, "My Fa-
> ther, if it is possible, take this cup of suffering
> from me! Yet not what I want, but what you
> want."
>
> Then he returned to the three disciples and
> found them asleep; and he said to Peter: *"How
> is it that you three were not able to keep watch
> with me for even one hour?* Keep watch and
> pray that you will not fall into temptation. The
> spirit is willing, but the flesh is weak."
>
> Once more Jesus went away and prayed, "My
> Father, if this cup of suffering cannot be taken
> away unless I drink it, your will be done." He
> returned once more and found the disciples
> asleep; they could not keep their eyes open.
>
> Again Jesus left them, went away, and prayed
> the third time, saying the same words. Then he
> returned to the disciples and said: "Are you still
> sleeping and resting? Look! The hour has come
> for the Son of Man to be handed over to the

power of sinful men. Get up, let us go. Look, here is the man who is betraying me!" (Matt. 26:36-46 TEV).

It is not possible to read this story without sensing the disappointment of Jesus. He had come to be with them, but they could not, for whatever reasons, remain with him. We are told that a few minutes later all the disciples ran away. But in a sense they had already departed. They withdrew from the quicksand of his choices and the anguish of his prayers and finally from the way of sorrows itself.

Perhaps that too was in the script. He went to his death sustained by the assurance that he had fulfilled his messianic destiny and comforted by the presence of the Father, but he seems to have gone unconsoled by those he had called to be his friends and brothers. At worst, they betrayed him; at best, they crept back to form a timid outer circle at the cross.

Relationships renewed

But out of the loneliness of Jesus and the refusal of his people to remain with him when the nature of his mission was to be with them, out of that messianic solitude, culminating in the cry of abandonment as well as of triumph on the cross, came a new community. Because Jesus was lonely for us in this final sense (which is really death in its most terrifying form), community and relationship have been made possible.

If the swimming motion of the arms (Eve reaching out and Adam reaching out to eat the fruit of

132

deathlessness) is the action underlying the desperation and warpedness, the atheism and poignancy of all civilizations, then the acceptance in the extended arms of Jesus on the cross speaks of his redemptive taking in of death for us and for our salvation.

He chose to die—and not because he was world-weary or morbid or grandiose. He hated and feared death and wanted to escape it. But he chose to die, because only in that way could he mend our broken relationship with God, the source of our life, and our relationships with one another, through which the life of God must flow.

He chose to die for me, for you. We read the tortuous and much disputed syntax of Hebrews 2:9: "But we see Jesus, who for a little while was made lower than the angels, crowned with glory and honor because of the suffering of death, *so that by the grace of God he might taste death for every one.*"

This is the gospel—the brief, stark, and infinitely good news of our salvation: "So that by the grace of God he might taste death for every one." The mystery of the first bloody hours is now being interpreted and made theologically clearer, but it remains no less a mystery.

The Greek of the New Testament rings like a great bell: *hopōs chariti theou hyper pantos geusētai thanatou.* Three hundred years later Jerome translated it into Latin: *ut gratia Dei pro omnibus gustaret mortem.*

Geusētai in Greek, as *gustaret* in Latin, means "he might taste" death. The word *tasting* is important. It is retained in the Revised Standard Version

133

but eliminated in *Good News for Modern Man*, presumably because it suggests savoring or nibbling, not eating. But the meaning of tasting in this context is to take something by mouth. The *Good News* rendering, "he should die for everyone," obliterates the coarse-grained truth that he took death into himself the way one takes food for nourishment and hence for life.

On that sunny day in Eden, when Eve, enraptured by the rhetoric of the serpent and magnetized by the attraction of the fruit—its shape, its smell, it promise of taste—stretched out her hand to take it and eat it and then gave some to her husband, she wanted to take immortality into herself. Instead she (whose name is *life*) and Adam tasted disobedience and death.

When Jesus cried out on the cross—speaking, according to Mark, in the messianic accents of Psalm 22—he tasted death. He let the bitter waters of mortality, which wash the farthest shores of our universe, course through him and mortify him.

He gave up the swimming motion, the ambition to start a new culture, a novel commonwealth that would prevail over Rome, or a new religion that would draw the multitudes to him and let him be the king of their hearts. He gave it all up and, after refusing the sponge soaked in drugged wine, which was raised to his lips, he gave the great shout, bowed his head, and died. It was an act, not of stoical resignation, but of tumultuous and perhaps reluctant obedience to his Father, to his mission, and to the Holy Spirit, which just then, like wind and fire, must

134

have swirled around him. Let us say, at least, that the obedience pulsated between reluctance and calm. The final peace came only when it was finished. *Consummatum est.*

In the moments of dying, the important thing was not what he felt (who could catalogue the passions of his Passion?) or how well he said what he needed to say, but only that, in the midst of the confusion and pain, he *obeyed.*

How can we describe his death? It was like an arrow flying true to the target, like a diver arching into the abyss, like a soldier hurling himself at the enemy, like a marathon runner flailing across the finish line.

It was like this, but it was more and different, for he who was both God and man gave up the desperate struggle to survive in the sea, not as a *tour de force,* but for us and our salvation. He committed himself to death, allowing it to engulf and overwhelm him, in order to remove its sting for us and the desperateness it arouses in us. And he did it as an act of mercy. Through the energy of the grace released by his death, he gave life back to us and us back to life.

But the life we got back was not the life we had given up, as we shall now see.

PART III

THE
RIGHT
TIME

TEN

THE
RIGHT
TIME

The death of Christ cannot be separated from his resurrection. It was, in fact, his being raised from the dead that preserved the Passion narrative and gradually pulled the gospels with it. In the most profound sense, the resurrection changed a human tragedy into "the divine comedy." Dante understood that better than his critics.

Thus, the earliest gospels are not so much biographies of Jesus as prefaces to the resurrection. Easter morning shines in all of them, perhaps most powerfully in the gospel of John, which presents a Jesus being robed in his glory, but unmistakably in the others as well.

The death and the resurrection were already present as a unit in the apostolic proclamation, the *kerygma*. That proclamation emerges in Acts, but Paul's version is our earliest written record. A quarter of a century after the events of the *kerygma*, Paul wrote to the believers in Corinth:

> And now, my brothers, I must remind you of the gospel that I preached to you; the gospel which

139

> you received, on which you have taken your
> stand, and which is now bringing you salvation.
> . . . First and foremost, I handed on to you the
> facts which had been imparted to me: that
> Christ died for our sins in accordance with the
> scriptures; that he was buried; that he was
> raised to life on the third day, according to the
> Scriptures (1 Cor. 15:1-4 NEB).

So the great drama is complete. Paul writes, "We know that Christ, once raised from the dead, is never to die again: he is no longer under the dominion of death" (Rom. 6:9 NEB).

But these triumphant words, like the blowing of a thousand trumpets, do not merely signal a victory in the cosmic salvation drama. They herald a totally new age and a new time for all people, people like you and me.

In the most ancient written source for the events surrounding the crucifixion of Christ, Paul's first letter to the church in Corinth, the death of Christ is identified with the slaying of the paschal lamb. Paul writes:

> It is not right for you to be proud! You know
> the saying, "A little bit of yeast makes the
> whole batch of dough rise." You must remove
> the old yeast of sin so that you will be entirely
> pure. Then you will be like a new batch of dough
> without any yeast, as indeed I know you actual-
> ly are. For our Passover Festival is ready, now
> that Christ, our Passover lamb, has been sacri-
> ficed. Let us celebrate our Passover, then, not
> with bread having the old yeast of sin and wick-
> edness, but with the bread that has no yeast, the
> bread of purity and truth (1 Cor. 5:6-8 TEV).

Paul and John seem to be drawing on the same original source, for John places the crucifixion on

140

Nisan 14, the very time when the paschal lambs would be sacrificed in preparation for the Passover feast, which began at sundown or 6 P.M.

This identification of Jesus with the paschal lamb and with the unleavened paschal bread is intended by the apostle, and certainly by the primitive church from which he derived it, to serve as a symbol of the mighty act of God in Christ which made time over, redeemed it, and invested it with an entirely new quality.

The new age

The resurrection heralds the dawning of a new age. It is impossible to read about the events surrounding the death, resurrection, and ascension of Jesus and Pentecost without sensing a mood of novelty and freshness. It is Easter morning! People are alive with an excitement resembling intoxication. A new love and a new intensity of existence leap like flame from person to person. There are new presuppositions and new possibilities for everything; new meaning lies like a fresh dew on the earth. And the Holy Spirit comes like a mighty wind to make all this a present possibility.

In *God's Grandeur,* Gerald Manley Hopkins says it poetically and thus comes closer to its meaning:

And for all this, nature is never spent:
There lives the dearest freshness deep down things;
And though the last lights off the black West went
Oh, morning at the brown brink eastward, springs—
Because the Holy Ghost over the bent
World broods with warm breast
  and with ah! bright wings.

The intent of all this is not to destroy history but to fulfill it, to bring it closer to the Creator's intention. The new day is not automated and routine, forced upon people against their will. Nor is it a state above history, as if by it the agony and the ecstasy of the first creation are nullified. In a sense, all things are as they were, and yet everything has the possibility of difference. Time is redeemed; time can be redeemed.

The messianic scenario, which Jesus consummated through his life, suffering, death, and resurrection, was an act of primal reconciliation. In Christ, God came to be with us and to heal broken relationships. The primal rupture had been the breaking of those relationships (with God, people, and creation) through an act of wanton isolation suggested by the serpent or the isolate Lucifer in the serpent. That original sin was followed by all the destructive and self-destructive action that soaks history in blood.

But the blood of Jesus cleanses from all sin and thus effects reconciliation and healed relationships. And through Holy Communion the blood of Jesus is taken in and circulates through persons and communities, through all the bodies of Christ, which are his body in the world.

New person, new community

The new creation is the new person now at peace with God and no longer an alien and a stranger. Through the redemptive act of Christ, the new persons are aware of who they are in relation to the

142

God who made them, in relation to themselves, and in relation to their intimates and the world. Through the redemptive work of Christ, these persons feel themselves to be totally accepted in an act of unconditional love (or grace) and able to accept themselves and others. Through redemption they also are able to delight in themselves, in others, and in God.

The new creation is also the new community, the *koinonia*, the family of grace. Within that family it is possible to meet all others as persons without reference to age, talent, skill, status, or power. In the family of grace, I live in growing awareness of the other and in increasing acceptance and delight of the other. In the family of grace I also become aware of the gifts of the Holy Spirit for ministry to the family and to the world.

But the new creation, whether in person or community, does not abolish the old. The new time does not mean that I am no longer a creature of time. The new time, in fact, makes me live my life in time with greater courtesy and charity. I take it more seriously, live more solemnly in it, seek its redemption with greater devotion. But I am also freer and merrier about it, for with the apostle Paul I am standing "on tiptoe to see the wonderful sight of the sons of God coming into their own" (Rom. 8:19 Phillips).

There have been times in the history of the church when the Holy Spirit seemed so present that time could be ignored. In such end-times, the ceremonies and festivals marking our passage through time, as well as other rituals, have been set aside. Even our life in the family of blood and in the day-to-day, living, working community has been set aside as being less spiritual or relevant than the life apart from life.

But such a devaluation of the old time violates the belief that it is precisely in time that redemption is to take place and new meaning be infused. Jesus went to the synagogue on the Sabbath, "as his custom was," and attended the temple festivals that were incumbent on him as an adult male in the Jewish community. The early Christian fellowship did not sever its connection with the temple observances until forced to do so, and even then proceeded to make them a part of its own worship.

Jesus made it quite clear that he came not to destroy the Law but to fulfill it. What this means practically is that both institutions and rituals are to be treated gently. They are not to serve as the ultimate meaning of our life and thus exercise a tyranny over us, but as far as possible, they are to be respected and used both as reminders of our humanity and our identity with the rest of creation and as means of coping with the pain as well as the joy of passage.

In an earlier part of this book, we tried to identify passages that have been ritualized in the past and those that have not been so ritualized but may need to be.

Against the background of the Jesus events and the new time, we now need to find fresh and effective ways in which both the experience of passage and the rituals used to deal with it can be interpreted and assimilated by the persons concerned. We also need to see how the experience of passage and ritual can serve the Christian *koinonia* as a means of healing and a background for witness.

Let us begin by reviewing what the church or churches now do with passage, what more needs to be done, and how it can be done most effectively.

How the church handles passages

The church deals ritually with those passages that have life-death import. Through its appointed clergy, the church is present at birth, puberty, marriage, the birth of children from the marriage, birthdays and anniversaries, crises brought on by illness or death, and finally at death itself.

The presence of the church is felt in the prescribed rituals for these occasions, but also in other ways. For example, the church has historically told and retold the life story of Jesus, who identified himself with our humanity by being born, growing to adulthood, forming and dissolving relationships, entering upon a career, pursuing the career through a series of successes and disappointments, facing opposition, and finally being put to death.

The church has also stressed that Christ was crucified and raised from the dead so that his resurrection power might be available to us in our daily life. It has emphasized that the risen Lord is our companion in crisis and transition, and that through the gift of prayer we may claim his presence and his power to help us deal with the pain of passage.

145

The church has done less well in identifying and ritualizing nontraditional passages. For example, churches that take a determined stand against divorce and remarriage can hardly be expected to ritualize these passages. But the church has also neglected passages in which no moral ambiguity exists.

Even with traditionally accepted and ritualized passages, the church could do more to interpret the meaning of the passage and to help people assimilate it. By *interpretation* I mean making the experience more understandable and acceptable; by *assimilation* I mean the process whereby an experience is positively integrated into one's life.

I think the church has been hesitant in these areas because it has assumed that the task of interpretation is largely theological and hence must be assigned to the professional clergy or at least to those theologically trained. It seems also to have believed that enabling assimilation is a matter for professional psychologists or other trained counselors—people who, alas, are in short supply.

Professionals can no doubt help people interpret and assimilate passages, but people also profit from the presence of others who listen with discernment, empathize, and truly care. We learn to accept the pain of passage by sharing it with people struggling with the same issues. We best assimilate it by finding support among a fellowship of carers.

Such interpretation and assimilation are clarified and reinforced and given transcendent meaning within the body of Christ, where the risen Lord is present. Ultimate meaning and blessing must come from him who has promised to be present where two or three are gathered in his name. It is consistent with our faith to believe that such meaning and blessing are communicated directly by the Lord as well as through members of his body.

Because we believe in the dynamic presence of Christ, we can intercede, invoking Christ's presence in the life of the person in passage. To intercede for a person is to confess that we cannot go it alone.

The powers of darkness

We need the Lord's presence not only because we are mortals and get tired, but because we are a garrison besieged by enemies. The dark powers of the universe are not indifferent to our pilgrimage. They know that each moment of passage moves us toward consummation or destruction. And even though the great victory has been won over them and they are chained, they retain the energy of evil and the capacity for harm.

To speak this way lays me open to the charge of having a medieval world view. The image of small demons invading our life and initiating misrule is ridiculous to me, but I find no way of eliminating Dostoevsky's "dread spirit, the spirit of self-destruction and non-existence." I find no fully developed theology of evil in the Scriptures—the incarnation of a malicious intent to match the incarnation of the divine Word—and it may well be, as Luther says, that the devil wheels dung in God's garden, and

147

hence that evil is not ultimate in a world where Christ has triumphed. Nevertheless, a description of life that omits the demonic is, at least in my experience, flat and unconvincing.

Perhaps that is why so many people in our time are ready to identify with literature that makes room for the "adversary." C. S. Lewis's *Screwtape Letters*, his Narnia books, and particularly his science fiction books are "tales of devilry," to use his own term. And on a grander scale, J. R. R. Tolkien's *The Hobbit* and *Lord of the Rings* make evil as palpable and inescapable as "the Land of Mordor where the shadows lie." Even debased versions of devilry and exorcism made popular in films and books make clear that people are looking not so much for a simpler view of life as for a view that will do justice to the darkness (and the light) that they sense in themselves and others.

Against this background, what is the role of prayer? Invoking the Lord's presence is more than inviting his observation or counsel. Through prayer we enlist the Lord as an ally in a life-and-death struggle against "the Devil and all his wiles," to quote the Book of Common Prayer. The situation is seen as harboring the energy, intelligence, and malice of incarnate evil as well as the incarnate power, wisdom, and love of God. Christians are sent forth to their pilgrimage and their struggle armored and armed for victory (Eph. 6:10-13).

Victory is not merely the achievement of moral conformity in the individual, nor is it the establishment of a cautious, respectable community in which

148

the anxiety of risk and the pain of growth are eliminated. Such "cloistered virtue" has often led to sterile moralism.

The old hymn line "He died to make us good" perpetuates the belief that the ideal Christian is the good person and the ideal community is the good community. Hence we ought to pray to be made good and we ought to pray for the goodness of others. But that standard easily deteriorates into a demand for superficial niceness. It encourages the repression, not only of discourtesy and malice, but also of personal freedom and creativity.

We are indebted to Freud and Jung for insight into the process of repression. We have learned that outward behavior cannot be taken at face value; it may serve to mask unacceptable feelings and motivations. Honesty is thus healthier than conformity, and it is the only condition out of which genuine love can flow.

What the psychologists tell us in technical language is what our Lord made apparent in his own life. Jesus saw the truth about himself and other people, and he was not frightened off. On the contrary, the more he saw of our reality, the more he loved us.

We must seek this kind of truthfulness in times of passage. The intercession we envisage is intended to do battle against every kind of falsehood and to evoke those deep charities that are the gift of Christ to those who trust him.

Christians concerned about being vulnerable and honest, Christians who want to care, confront, affirm, and celebrate will welcome opportunities to be available to friends in their transitional crises and will, in turn, seek such help themselves. In such an atmosphere we can work through pain and welcome joy together. When the body of Christ enters into experiences of passage, the experiences serve as opportunities for renewing faith and love in the fellowship.

Processing passages

In the pages that follow there is a sampling of common passages and suggestions for dealing with them. I have not tried to write new formal rituals or to rewrite old ones. I believe this task will have to be done, but priority must now be given to processing passages. When no appropriate rituals exist, they will have to be improvised.

For the following scenarios, I have assumed certain circumstances: that the persons involved have formal or informal connections with the institutional church, that in these churches there are both professional and nonprofessional persons of sensitivity who are willing to share insights and feelings with those involved in critical transition, that small groups ready to process the grist of experience exist or can readily be formed, that those involved are willing to innovate and take risks, and that there is an openness toward the working of the Holy Spirit in individuals and groups.

Pastors and other professionals have a unique role in processing passages. They help to create the atmosphere of trust and caring in which the process is carried out. They also provide guidelines and procedures to increase the skill and confidence of the lay persons entrusted with the process. But in any but the smallest parish, the pastor cannot be present for all times of passage. It may also be undesirable to lay responsibility for processing passages entirely on the pastor's shoulders; the pastor's participation may become routine and perfunctory. Lay persons need opportunities to risk and grow and to be priests for one another.

ELEVEN

BEGINNINGS

Rituals of birth and beginning are already available in most Christian churches. They are either the baptism (or christening) of infants (with a range of theological interpretations) or their dedication to God without the use of water. Dedication seems to be a ritual developed in analogy to infant baptism and derived from Old Testament modes such as presentation and consecration and from our Lord's blessing of the children.

These rituals, whether baptisms or dedications, have deep historic and religious meaning. Hence they ought not be treated as a mere formality but should be interpreted and assimilated by the families involved.

What we envisage, in addition to the rite itself and its formal interpretation by a pastor as part of the service in the public sanctuary, is a time of more intimate sharing of ideas and feelings by the family and friends of the child. Perhaps such sharing, which provides opportunities for interpreting, assimilating, and interceding, can best be done as part of the home celebration after the public service.

Interpretation

The search for particular meaning in this ritual experience will include remembering, reflecting on the Scriptures, and focusing on insights that the day has brought.

1. Remembering   Sharing personal and family memories about the birth ritual will clarify its significance. Looking at certificates, Bibles, and other mementos in which the birth rituals of other members of the family are mentioned will underline the day's meaning.

2. Reflecting on the Scriptures   The base of recollection is widened and deepened by thinking together about some of the biblical birth stories. Those of Isaac, Samson, Samuel, and John the Baptist provide us with an awesome sense of God's design and compassion. The story of Jesus' birth intertwines glory and peril.

The sense of God's presence in the birth of a child is strengthened by reading passages such as Psalm 139:13-18, which make possible personal identification with the biblical word. The sense of God's involvement in my being born can be joyous and affirming, but also awesome and sobering.

3. Identifying learnings   Interpreting also involves distilling out particular insights that the day has brought. The following questions may help to provide focus:

In what way does today's ceremony serve to make the child a part of the community of faith?

What have we learned from having this child in our midst?

How can we accept the child as a child and encourage its learning and growing without forgetting that we need to be converted and become like children?

Assimilation

Interpreting is largely a "head trip" and needs to be supplemented by sharing feelings. The following questions may help this process:

How has this rite of passage affected us as parents of the child? Do we feel secure and happy about having entrusted this child in a special way to God's care? What feelings other than of thankfulness and joy are we feeling: worry, tiredness, grief, depression, and even guilt and envy?

If there are other children in the family, how are they responding to this event? Do they feel a part of the experience of welcoming the new child or excluded from it?

What are the feelings of the extended family (uncles, aunts, cousins, grandparents, sponsors or godparents, and other significant persons outside the family)? What role, if any, do they see themselves playing in relation to the child?

Intercession

If, indeed, we have to confront "the Devil's evil tricks" (Eph. 6:11 TEV) from the beginning of our lives, our prayer for the child becomes a counterattack against a determined enemy.

In the Narnia books by C. S. Lewis, Aslan, the

Lion, is a Christ-figure. He is seen as "the guardian of souls," which, translated into modern language, means the protector of our identity. In praying for the child, this should be kept in mind. We pray for those gifts that will make the child not only healthy and attractive, but also whole and strong "in the Lord" and thus victorious against all forces that undermine integrity.

Such integrity cannot be separated from self-awareness and self-acceptance, for strength does not flow from distrust, and hatred of self, but from accepting oneself in the presence of Christ. From security of this kind will come healthy self-love and the capacity to love others and God.

Praying for the child might hence take the following form: Those present spend a few minutes in quiet reflection on what spiritual gifts they would like to give the child. They then form a circle symbolizing their desire to be *with* the child in love and acceptance. In prayers of one word, they give their gifts.

The prayers may take the following form. First the leader says, "Father, we thank you for _____, who has been baptized (or dedicated) today. Aware of the great blessing of life as well as its real perils, we would prayerfully offer the following gifts to him/her."

Particular words are then spoken: kindness . . . wholeness . . . strength . . . discernment . . . truthfulness . . . blessedness . . . security . . . hopefulness . . . warmth . . . courage, etc. Each person who prays may come back into the prayer as often as desired.

The prayers may be concluded by singing the verse of a song such as "Alleluia," "What a Friend We Have in Jesus," "Blest Be the Tie That Binds," or the doxology.

TWELVE

GROWING UP

In churches that practice the baptism of infants, confirmation typically follows. In addition to its educational role (which is substantial in some Christian churches), this ceremony functions as a puberty rite, welcoming the child into the adult community.

In churches that dedicate infants and immerse young people when they reach the age of accountability, immersion functions as a puberty rite. Although the age of immersion varies greatly, the intent of the rite is typically to usher the child into the adult fellowship of the church. It is assumed that the child is now old enough to discern options and to make a conscious commitment. The baptism of President and Mrs. Carter's daughter Amy at the age of nine was reported in the press as an occasion on which she was invited to confess her personal experience of the new birth and her understanding of what this involved for her as a responsible person.

The rites attendant to growing up also need a more personal interpretation and assimilation than can be provided in the scheduled activities of the

157

church. Hence a scenario for such a process is suggested. The young person involved in the ceremony should be given an opportunity to assent to the process and to share in planning it.

On the day of the rite, or closely associated with it, family members and friends who have a special interest in the young person may be invited to a time of sharing. Two or three confirmands or candidates for baptism may be more comfortable experiencing the processing together, but involving too many young people may serve to blur the intensely personal focus of the event.

Interpretation

Why confirmation? This question troubles both present and former confirmands. In some churches it is the subject of discussion among clergy, parents, and children before the course begins, but a more personal critique of the process after it is over may be helpful.

A discussion of confirmation (or of adult baptism if that is appropriate) might begin most comfortably by devoting some time to remembering and history-giving. In reflecting on the ceremony, those present share briefly their own memories and traditions, including both serious and comic elements. A guiding question might be: What one good happening or learning or relationship from my own confirmation has stayed with me? Such a procedure may free the present confirmands to enter into the discussion, which we hope will move toward a consensus on the value of the training.

If confirmation is a "growing up" experience, it may be appropriate to reflect briefly on scripture passages dealing with growing up (for example, the stories of Joseph and David). It seems that biblical children moved to adulthood very rapidly, whereas in our day the transition is much slower.

This may lead to the question of how confirmation or adult baptism changes the young people's relationship to the church. Are they now ready for more freedom and responsibility than the faith community is ready to grant?

Assimilation

This is also a time for those involved to vent their feelings. The young people should be invited to express elation, pride, relief, and thankfulness as well as guilt, frustration, anger, boredom, and grief.

Questions such as the following may be helpful: What in the experience of confirmation or preparation for baptism did I find most comfortable, rewarding, exciting, helpful? What did I find most difficult, painful, trying? What is my feeling now that the experience is over? (The questions may be handed out earlier to give the young people a chance to reflect and to write out their answers.)

The parents will also feel relief, satisfaction, gratitude, and pride as well as frustration, disappointment, and guilt. They may want to ask: What was most helpful to our child and to me in the experience? What had more limited value? What was particularly burdensome to me and our family? What was rewarding? What hopes do we have for our child and for our family as a result of this experience?

Intercession

Intercession may take several forms. The group may want to form a circle around the young person and have several or all members of the group pray briefly and specifically for the young person's concerns as revealed in the responses to the questions.

The group may prefer to divide into twos. Each person may share a specific concern, and the other person commits that concern to God.

The intent of this prayer time is to invoke the presence of God as well as to demonstrate caring. It may also serve to incorporate the young person into the ongoing fellowship.

THIRTEEN

JOINING UP

In a world that, for better or worse, is becoming more Western, urban, industrial, and commercial, the most important passage is often the termination of compulsory education and the beginning of advanced training or some form of military or social service. This is the time of joining up, of accepting one's place in society.

For many young people in the United States, the time of growing up has been further extended. Joining up comes at the end of college. For many years American colleges and universities have functioned *in loco parentis* (in the place of the parent), and until graduation the young person has been, in the language of the apostle Paul, "under tutors and governors." The turmoil of the '60s changed all that, and now more and more young people are becoming responsible for themselves at an earlier time.

Rituals

Closure has always been important to me, and as I write this, a very painful memory of my own leave-taking from home surfaces. A brother, four years older than I, left home for college. Young people from our church gathered at the house. There were speeches, games, a gift. Most important, my father shared some very deep feelings about what my brother's going meant to him. He even wept some rare tears. I was moved by the experience and entered into my father's grief.

Some years later it was my turn to leave for college, and the event was hardly noticed. There was neither party nor gift, which caused me a lot of pain, but worst of all there was no real closure with my family. Until the last minute, I hoped for something, but nothing occurred.

I do not record this memory out of self-pity. My home was exceptionally warm and supportive, and I am sure circumstances accounted for the omission of a rite of closure. I mention it only to stress how important closures are for young people, however self-reliant and assured they may seem.

Ritualizing this passage, at the end of high school or college, is now largely a secular function carried out by the schools. Many graduation exercises in the United States continue to include a wan gesture toward formal religion, and some churches make an effort to recognize graduates at public worship, but the transitional ceremony is no longer in the sole keeping of the faith community. If young people are to benefit from the insights and support of the churches at this passage, there will have to be a more personal scenario to supplement the rite of the schools.

Since this occasion signals the end of parental control, the role of the family in arranging for it will depend on the wishes of the young people being honored. They will have their own ceremonies of closure with their intimate peer group, but it is quite possible that they will also welcome an occasion of thanksgiving and blessing with their family or extended family, if such an occasion is understood to be an expression of love and caring.

Interpretation

The format of this occasion will vary from family to family, but it will probably include elements of recollection, and, depending on the interests of the family, some identification with biblical drama, especially with the life of our Lord. It may be helpful to remember that Jesus had a painful separation from his own family (Mark 3:31-35) and from his community (Luke 4:16-30). For Jesus, the freedom to "do his own thing"—a freedom most young people covet—brought him not only the exhilaration of his baptism at the hand of John and the dramatic visitation of the Holy Spirit, but a grim encounter with the devil in the wilderness.

The mood of the closure is thus not simply happy (although it is certainly that) but a mixture of the solemn, the joyous, the worrisome, the poignant, and the comic. "So sad, so fresh, the days that are no more."

Young people should be encouraged to share both their memories and their hopes without being put down or patronized. This is the time for them to interpret what the passage means in terms of their immediate plans as well as their long-term ambitions.

Assimilation

Such sharing may lead naturally to the entire family revealing their feelings. Every passage has a profound effect on family dynamics, and it is helpful to share grief and anxiety as well as thankfulness, elation, and pride. The young person will be honored if family members identify their feelings and try to express them.

The following questions may be helpful: What one gift, among many that I received from _____'s presence in our family, am I particularly thankful for? What one feeling among many (grief, nostalgia, anxiety, guilt, loneliness) am I having difficulty dealing with right now?

The person being honored may want to respond to similar questions: For what one gift that I have received in this family am I especially grateful? What am I feeling right now that I would like to share?

FOURTEEN

UNITING IN MARRIAGE

Uniting in marriage and assuming the responsibilities of family life once signaled stability and continuity in our social order. It is characteristic of our time that the marriage contract has now become more tenuous than vocational commitment. A few decades ago marriage was assumed to be permanent. There were casualties, of course, and these grew in number with the coming of World War II, but people said "until death do us part" with great seriousness, even if they had little or no Christian commitment.

For a time, as the divorce rates grew alarmingly, it was assumed, as is usual in American society, that the problems of marriage would yield to improved education in the schools and more effective counseling. Pastors and professional counselors were hence called upon for crisis intervention. Although these efforts were well-intentioned and professionally competent, the trend toward impermanence was not reversed. Even within faith communities, marriages were eroding. The solemnization of marriage, though outwardly no less ceremonial, seemed to carry with

165

it a mental reservation, a built-in escape hatch in the event things did not work out.

There was a time when the legally and socially structured institution of marriage could stand on its own and the church's role could be limited to blessing the union. It is now apparent that churches must serve as more than ceremonial agents. They must support realistic programs such as Marriage Enrichment and Marriage Encounter. They must advocate marriage as a form of fidelity to God and to the values of personhood and personal relations, while retaining their freedom to mediate grace and acceptance to those who, for seemingly valid reasons, may need to reconsider their commitment.

This is not a happy position for the churches. It would be a great deal easier if the churches could simply stand on dogma or wash their hands of the messy complexities of marriage by proclaiming it a civil contract. Such options are not available, for churches must live in the midst of the ambiguities of life's struggles and, in obedience to their Lord, provide guidance and support for people in every situation, including the vexing one of marriage.

The following scenario is intended, not as a major cure for the ailments of marriage, but as a means of helping people understand and integrate this significant passage.

Ritual

In many Christian churches, traditional wedding ceremonies prescribe roles for the bride and groom.

Such historical rituals certainly have their value, but a case can also be made for allowing the bride and groom a freer hand in fashioning the service, so they become genuine participants.

Perhaps the marriage ceremony would benefit, if not in style at least in integrity, if the bride and groom had the opportunity to think through and write their own vows in order to better understand the contract to which they are committing themselves. For marriage is a passage much more significant and irreversible than is imagined. In spite of all the provisions for its dissolution in today's society, it should not be lightly entered into. In a very special way it makes two people into one flesh, and the tearing of that flesh, no matter what the provocations and justifications may be, always leaves scar tissue.

Interpretation

Where, in the hurly-burly of prewedding activities—showers, breakfasts, dinners, receptions, car and plane arrivals, motel reservations, displaying of gifts—is there occasion for meaningful reflection on what is happening? Perhaps a better time to reflect on implications of this passage is after the honeymoon and housewarmings are past. The reflective process may best take place in the family of grace, that is, friends outside the family of blood who are willing to share insights and feelings. Such a group should probably be composed of recently married

167

couples, with an experienced couple acting as catalysts.

Reflection on the meaning of the marriage just celebrated might well begin with participants recalling experiences from their own families. The following questions may provide guidelines:

What was it like for me to grow up in a family as the only child or one of several? What were some happy times I had with parents and siblings? What tensions that I hoped would be resolved weren't?

What did married life seem to be like for the people I observed—parents, relatives, friends, neighbors? Did these people seem to stick to marriage because it was "the thing to do"?

The Christian faith seems to take marriage very seriously. (See Matthew 5:27-32, 19:1-11; Mark 10:1-12; Luke 16:18; 1 Corinthians 7.) How important is this for me in thinking about my marriage?

Assimilation

Such clarification of values may open the door to sharing deeper feelings related to marriage. The group may want to share questions such as the following:

For me the most satisfying thing about leaving home and setting up our own household was _____

_____. The most difficult thing was _____.

For me the most important comfort/joy of marriage, aside from sexual intimacy, is:

168

_____ the opportunity to be myself and to be accountable only to my spouse (that is, a peer person)

_____ to have a place that is really my own

_____ feeling that the future is going to be more
stable than the past, yet with many exciting
changes

_____ the prospect of having children

_____ not being lonely in the same way

_____ the chance to share my faith with someone I
love most of all

For me one of the difficulties of being married is:

_____ the expectation that we not let our marriage
fail

_____ some people's belief that conflict in our marriage is unchristian

_____ some people's belief that in a Christian marriage the wife must always be submissive and
the husband dominant

_____ the feeling I sometimes get that I can never be
a child but must always be a super-responsible
adult

_____ some people's belief that when you are married
no member of the opposite sex can be attractive
to you

Intercession

If more than three couples are present, it may be
helpful to divide into groups of four and have each

person restate his or her major concern. After some time for clarification, each person in the group prays specifically for the concerns of the person to his or her right until all have been included.

FIFTEEN

GOING AWAY

We come now to the most difficult of our scenarios: one for people who, without wanting a rupture with the Christian faith and community, choose to question, postpone, or perhaps reject a conventional way of life. To this category belong:

1. Singles who choose to remain that way
2. The divorced
3. Those who choose some form of collective living
4. Those who follow an atypical career

The decision to adopt one of these life-styles is a passage with serious implications for the future.

Singles　　Because of the strong impact of Luther and other reformers who made a virtue of marriage and family life in reaction to Roman Catholic celibacy, Protestants have tended to see the fulfillment of life as inevitably associated with marriage. Although there is no theoretical bias against singleness or deliberate celibacy, these states are distrusted as being not quite normal. This is one of several instances in which traditional behavior and Christian norms get confused. The assumption seems to be that white, middle-class, Protestant norms can be simply equated with Christian ideals. The result has been our isolation from Christians with a life-style different from our own.

In Matthew 19:12 (TEV) Jesus says, "For there are different reasons why men cannot marry: some, because they were born that way; others, because men made them that way; and others do not marry for the sake of the Kingdom of heaven." The meaning of this passage is not entirely clear. In reporting it the evangelist may have reflected some of the questions the primitive church had about the unmarried state. These questions emerged very early, as is evidenced by the apostle Paul's discussion of them in 1 Corinthians 7.

But whether or not this is so, Jesus certainly makes room for people who, for whatever reason, natural or spiritual, do not marry. Despite the strong emphasis on marriage in the mainstream of Judaism, Jesus himself was not married, and the apostle Paul was certainly not married, at least at the time of his missionary labors.[1]

There is hence nothing patronizing or pitying in the statement of our Lord relative to single people. Apparently both Jesus and Paul saw singleness as a condition for their own ministry. In our day it may be a condition for an optional life-style and deserves to be so considered.

The Divorced   There is a category of singles that poses a special problem for the church: those who, without evidence of unfaithfulness in their married partner but for other reasons valid to them, proceed to end their marriage in legal separation or divorce.

Because Christian marriage is, according to the words of our Lord and the tradition of the primitive church, a contract binding for life, the divorce of Christians has historically been looked upon as evidence of moral failure and of the absence of true spirituality. But with the dramatic increase in the number of divorces even within the faith community, this stance must be examined.

So long as churches seek to be faithful to the word of Jesus as revealed in the Scriptures, the dissolution of a marriage cannot be seen merely as the cancellation of a contract, mutually satisfactory to both parties. Christian marriage is a covenant "in the Lord"—a solemn agreement entered into in his presence and with his blessing. Hence its strength and permanence derive not from its institutional but from its spiritual character. The parties are joined in the Lord's presence and they continue their married life in that presence; any dissolution of the union must be enacted in his presence.

But how and when is a dissolution justified if the very nature of marriage is permanence during the tenure of mortal life, that is, "until death do us part"?

At one level it is not justified. Our Lord unquestionably saw it as permanent. "Man must not separate, then, what God has joined together" (Matt. 19:6 TEV).

Jesus was speaking in response to his adversaries,

who cited the commandment of Moses that a certificate of divorce be given the woman. Jesus argued that this provision was made "for your hardness of heart." In much of the Semitic world, the initiative for divorce rested entirely with the man. He could arbitrarily end a marriage and leave his wife with almost no recourse. But a certificate of divorce, enjoined by the mosaic law, gave her freedom to remarry without fear of any harassment from her former husband. This was infinitely more just than the procedure then current, a procedure reflecting "hardness of heart."

But Jesus came to bring in a new dispensation that would show even more consideration for the personhood of the woman than did the mosaic law. Wives may now be assured that no arbitrary act on the part of the husband, though duly certified according to the law of Moses, can cast them out of the marriage. They are indissolubly a part of it.

The reason for our Lord's position is, I believe, his concern for the creation in general and for human beings in particular. He expressed concern especially for those who, out of their defenselessness, become the victims of cruelty and injustice.

What I believe this means, in substance, is that the rightness or wrongness of divorce, or of marriage for that matter, depends in the final analysis not on a propositional truth but on what happens to the persons involved. Jesus said that the Sabbath was made for people and not people for the Sabbath. Marriage was ordained by God to give the matrix of the human family stability and permanence. But both the Sabbath and marriage were ordained by God *for* people. When they do not serve that purpose, an even higher law must be appealed to.

There are people who imperil their personhood by remaining in an impossible marriage, and there are people who do violence to their own personhood and that of their spouse and children by terminating a marriage that, by some tending and caring, might be raised to newness of life. The church, in obedience to its Lord, has the responsibility to encourage and enable faithful and stable marriages. It also has a responsibility to stand with and to minister to persons for whom such an option does not seem to exist.

Collectives   Another category of nontraditional life-style is found in collectives or communes. Very often such living is in reaction to the restrictions of the nuclear family. Many collectives represent an effort to create an extended family in accordance with Christian principles and some of the procedures of the Jerusalem church (Acts 2:44-47, 4:32-35, 5:1-11).

Communal living has been carried out by so many different groups with such diversity of objectives and procedures that even Christian collectives may be seen as a threat to the traditional community. But they are the implementation of dreams and hopes of sincere Christians who are looking for a way to make the gospel relevant to the world we live in. Hence, they deserve to be listened to and to be considered a valid part of the family of faith. The transition from a more conventional life-style to a collective, with its risks, trials, and rewards, is a

175

passage calling for an appropriate ritual as well as process.

Unusual careers   The fourth category of non-conformity involves those persons who renounce the "Protestant work ethic" and choose to live and function with different motivations than those provided by our economic system. They often live outside that system, insofar as that is possible. Some opt for working minimally or not at all. Others work at a craft, a trade, or an art whose primary compensations are other than financial. The eschatological mood about these activities reminds us of Paul's injunction in 1 Corinthians:

> What I mean, my brothers, is this: there is not much time left, and from now on married men should live as though they were not married; those who weep, as though they were not sad; those who laugh, as though they were not happy; those who buy, as though they did not own what they bought; those who deal in material goods, as though they were not fully occupied with them. For this world, as it is now, will not last much longer (1 Cor. 7:29-31 TEV).

I think the apostle is saying that most people spend their energy trying to make the world order more substantial, so that it will not be torn from them by the galactic winds beginning to hum in the rigging—hence the overseriousness about marriage, tears, laughter, commerce, worldly goods, etc. But Christians ought to let the worldly riggings thin out and become porous. Thus they will be receptive to the new order beginning to pour in.

Those who argue for a different career style have some of this spirit. They see the present world order

176

passing away and something new coming. But unlike Paul and the primitive church, they are freer and more playful in their approach to existence. They are inclined to live in the now, to claim the blessing of the temporary, to "let their child out" in play and frolic, and not to be overwhelmed by the cares and riches of this world.

To those of us who have been conditioned to dictums such as "idle hands are the devil's workshop," "work, for the night is coming," or "killing time is a form of murder," such free behavior is threatening and we may be inclined to feel that it is unspiritual. But it too deserves a hearing that is accepting and unpatronizing.

Rituals

Relatively few rituals exist for the passages in which nonconventional decisions involve us. In the Roman Catholic Church, entering upon a religious vocation has been associated with ceremonial designs that are the products of centuries of experience and reflection. But I know of no Protestant ritual that recognizes celibacy, whether temporary or permanent.

Some churches are now at work developing ceremonies for the termination of marriages and some individuals have improvised closures. A friend, involved in a painful divorce after a decade of marriage, responded to my question about a ritual by saying that even without any conscious awareness of what they were doing, he and his wife shared the news about their separation with their children before the fireplace in the living room. This is where they had experienced their unity and joy as a family, and to this place they returned to grieve. He was reminded, he said, of a tradition in his home town in the South. Funeral services were held, not in the church or in the funeral parlor, but in the front parlor of the home. Here the family had celebrated life; here they gathered to say good-bye and to work through the passage death had brought.

But even though the need for closure is now being recognized, relatively little is being done. Despite such poverty of ceremony, churches continue to have a stake in the life and nurture of their nontraditional members, not only because the churches have something to say to them, but also because such members may provide a needed stimulus for the life and thought of the churches. Hence the churches must struggle to develop particular rites and scenarios for those involved in passages, even when this puts a strain on both energy and inventiveness.

Interpretation

Writing and staging a scenario for nonconforming Christians may be interpreted as manipulation. Accommodation to the needs and interests of nontraditional members may suggest that the churches are being "nice" in the hope that nonconformity will be changed into conformity and we shall live happily together ever after. But we are not talking about white hats and black hats, ins and outs, rights and

178

wrongs. We are simply honoring existing church boundaries and pushing out of our little enclaves to meet them. The life of the church involves interacting ministries under the lordship of Christ. We all have much to get from one another and much to give to one another.

Hence, I recommend the organization of small groups around the theme of "life options and decisions" without an effort to isolate any category of conformity or nonconformity.

The four passages involved in this scenario all require choice. Though occurring in time, they are not imposed on us by time. They are the result of consciously choosing one life-style in preference to another. Such choices inevitably raise the question of values.

In this situation interpretation inevitably means clarifying the difference between tradition and principle. Tradition is the standards of behavior imposed on us by the past, which may or may not contain value elements. Principles are the standards that flow inevitably from a value system we have adopted as our own. Traditional standards we call "dictums." Standards determined by values are "guidelines." Both dictums and guidelines generate guilt, but in the former case the guilt is largely false or unreal; in the latter, largely real.

The culture in which I grew up demanded that we "dress up" for church. I had one good suit, which I saved for church and other festive occasions. It would not have occurred to me to go to church in shirtsleeves or with unshined shoes. Such a demand

179

was obviously a dictum, since it had very little to do with the spirit in which I attended worship. But departing from this kind of dress still makes me feel guilty and ill at ease.

In going to church, however, I was aware of another kind of guilt that could not be "dressed" away. This had to do with my failure to be obedient to the will of God. In Matthew 23:23 Jesus draws a sharp line between what we have called dictums and guidelines. He is addressing the religious leaders of his day: "You give to God one tenth even of the seasoning herbs, such as mint, dill, and cumin, but you neglect to obey the really important teachings of the Law, such as justice and mercy and honesty" (TEV).

In clarifying behavior in terms of these distinctions, everyone will have an opportunity to analyze his or her choices and to deal with questions of discomfort and guilt.

Assimilation

Such a relaxed and nonjudgmental reflection on life issues may lead quite naturally to sharing feelings without fear of being misunderstood or rejected. It may clarify the difference between reactive and responsive behavior, that is, between behavior motivated by the need to punish or get even with those in authority and behavior growing out of a desire to be a good steward of one's life.

The heart of the matter, here as elsewhere, is the relationship between my decisions and actions and

180

the degree of my self-authentication. Do I come out feeling good about who I am? Am I willing to know myself and accept myself and even delight in myself because God has known me and accepted me and delights in me? And am I able to accept and delight in the persons around me?

Intercession

The situation calls for spontaneous prayer among the group participants, with particular needs and concerns of the moment given priority. People praying realistically for their own needs as well as the particular needs of others will create a climate of support and caring that is immeasurably strengthening for those in transition.

SIXTEEN

WINNING

A much-too-simple conclusion about American culture is that it breeds competitiveness and the need to win. The assumption seems to be that the need to win is an effect of which our society is a cause; it is not the outworking of a basic human drive. But biblical faith assures us that the need to control—even to control God—goes back to the beginning. And Abraham Maslow argues that, in the hierarchy of human needs, ego-status or esteem needs hold a prominent place.

In our money-oriented society, the rewards for winning are often associated with financial gain. But even in Soviet Russia, where one presumably "gives according to ability and takes according to need" (Marx), the need to win is undiminished.

In a hotel restaurant in Leningrad, I recently came upon a celebration that apparently had drawn together the area's VIPs. On their civilian jackets the Soviet leaders wore rows of ribbons and decorations rivaling the "fruit salad" on the uniformed chest of an American four-star general. And on many public buildings we saw 20-foot-high portraits of Lenin and more contemporary Russian power figures. Browning may have bewailed William Wordsworth's acceptance of the position of poet laureate in "The Lost Leader," but for most of us a ribbon "to stick in our coat" is hard to resist.

In his *Rhetoric* Aristotle writes: "While they [young men] love honor, they love victory still more; for youth is eager for superiority over others, and victory is one form of this. They love both more than they love money, which indeed they love very little, not having yet learned what it means to be without it" (Book 2, Chapter 12).

Our world differs little from that of Athens in the fourth century B.C. Whether the prize be honor or money, the pace to attain it has not decreased. If anything, young people today feel pressed to win earlier. They seem to feel that all is lost if they have not attained their summit by 40. And the mass media encourage this conviction. Hence the hysteric momentum one senses around academic institutions and financial and bureaucratic centers. There seems to be so little time in which to win a perishable crown.

Churches may want to stress the perils of this fever and to support those who follow another route, but they probably cannot do much to eliminate the phenomenon. A more realistic role for the churches is probably to minister to people where they are.

This raises the central question: How can the churches be helpful in the passage of winning? How

183

can it minister to those who achieve a highly desirable objective such as a doctoral degree; a coveted prize or award; an appointment or promotion to a significant level of leadership in business, labor union, government office, school, or military service; a victory in an election to public office; the acceptance of a book or article for publication?

Ritual

It is doubtful if the church needs to recognize these occasions with any formal ceremony, since our society is skillful in the rituals by means of which it confers its honors. But the church does need to develop scenarios to help individuals and their families and friends deal with the total impact of winning. Winning may be easier than losing, but it is not easy.

When I was a high school student, Rudyard Kipling's muscular idealism was much in vogue and several of us memorized the aphoristic wisdom of "If." The other day, out of absolutely nowhere came the lines:

> If you can meet with Triumph and Disaster
> And treat those two impostors just the same.

Why, of course. That was how I was taught to deal with both winning and losing. Get above them! Keep a stiff upper lip! Don't let anyone know how pleased you are or how destroyed!

But this won't do, even in winning, for to get

184

above something means to push it down and not allow yourself to feel either elation or depression—and both are there, for winning is a mixed bag and never just exhilarating. In addition to pride, relief, and wild gladness, it may bring disappointment (that the bang isn't bigger), grief, anger, depression, guilt, and anxiety.

A young man close to our family was, during his high school and college careers, a very competent and successful swimmer. He tells about a phenomenon frequently experienced and discussed in the locker room after a meet, especially a successful one—post-meet depression.

Alexander the Great, according to legend, wept because there were no more worlds to conquer, and it is an unhappy David we meet in the story of Bathsheba: a king who has conquered most of his enemies and who now languishes, bored, guilty, restless, and depressed in the city of his triumph, Jerusalem, the city of peace.

A psychologist friend found these symptoms in a successful candidate for the office of judge. All through law school and a distinguished law career this man had longed to crown his public life with a prestigious judgeship. He worked very hard to achieve it, overcame strong opposition, and finally won his place. But as soon as the judgeship was in the bag, he became seriously depressed and had to seek professional help.

Winning is a passage. Hence it needs its scenario and its process.

Interpretation

In a small group of caring and sensitive people, I, as a winner, may want to walk through the significant steps in my achievement. Was this something I have wanted for a long time? What were the obstacles and difficulties in reaching my goal? What resources did I have going for me, and what persons were particularly helpful?

Or maybe winning came as a surprise, and I need to think about it in those terms. Whatever the circumstances, I may want to ask how this experience fits into the overall design of my life and my ambitions and dreams.

This may be the time to talk frankly about achievement in terms of Christian values. Paul urges the Thessalonians (1 Thess. 4:11 Phillips), "Make it your ambition to have no ambition!" Does the apostle strike us as a person without ambition? And what about Jesus? How do we interpret his temptations in the wilderness? What form did ambition take for him?

Assimilation

These questions lead naturally into the area of feelings. Without allowing myself to be pressured, I may want to respond to the following questions:

What particular feelings do I feel right now? How much of what has happened to me can I claim as my achievement (with due allowance for distortion, of course) and how much do I need to credit to someone else? (Abraham Lincoln is supposed to have said, "All that I am or hope to be I owe to my angel mother.")

On the assumption that there is no "free lunch," what price do I see myself paying for this recognition? Will added expectations be imposed on me, as well as added commitments and responsibilities? How do I feel about that?

A poignant example of the price of glory is the experience of J. R. R. Tolkien after his *Lord of the Rings* became popular. One of his biographers reports that the harassment Tolkien and his family suffered from autograph seekers, relic hunters, and amateur photographers was so acute that they had to leave Oxford, where they had lived for several decades, and seek peace and anonymity in Bournemouth.

Often a spouse or associate has played a significant role in the work lying behind the achievement. This scenario provides them with an opportunity to ventilate feelings and to be heard. If you are in that position, you may want to respond to the following questions:

What am I feeling right now—elation, gratification, disappointment, envy, resentment? How much responsibility for _____'s achievement am I able to accept? Assuming that my relationship with the "winner" is more or less permanent, to what kind of future does _____'s achievement commit me?

Intercession

Some specific grounds for thankfulness as well as some particular needs and concerns will have emerged in the sharing process. These can be made the focus of brief personal prayers aimed at assuring the "winner" that he or she has a place in the group and is the object of ongoing love and caring.

SEVENTEEN

LOSING

Losing may be an "impostor" to Kipling, but for most of us it has a great deal of substance and truth. Hence, when we lose, our instinct is not to seek the company of people but to go away and hide. In 1952 after Adlai Stevenson had lost the presidential election to Dwight Eisenhower, he was interviewed briefly on television. When he was asked how he felt about losing, he said that it reminded him of what he had once heard a little boy say after he stubbed his toe: "I am too old to cry, and it hurts too much to laugh." Watching the program, I had the impression that Stevenson didn't want to be there at all; he wanted to find a quiet, dark place where he could lick his wounds.

The wounding of the ego, even in a small way, has the effect of undermining our total self-esteem. Some years ago Sidney Harris, the well-known columnist for the *Chicago Daily News*, admitted publicly that he assimilated, as a matter of course, the news that his column had been bought by a prestigious metropolitan daily, whereas the knowledge

189

that a small provincial paper had dropped his articles filled him with torment. It would seem that our ego esteem is so frail a craft that the slightest wave will capsize it.

Some years ago I wrote and had published a book on which I had staked some unrealistic hopes. It received some good reviews and some fair ones, but I did not qualify for any prize, nor did its sales reach my expectations. But what I remember especially about the book was the rage I felt and expressed when one reviewer said some very negative things about it. Like the impotent Lear raving on the heath and vowing revenge on his disloyal daughters, I plotted the total humiliation of the reviewer in any future encounter with him.

I can't forget the dismay of one of our children at this display of temper. She found it terrifying, as if I had suddenly gone mad. And, of course, I had. Someone had presumed to prick the balloon of my ego, and I was out of control, like a child in a tantrum.

When we fail, we probably need to ask ourselves to what degree our status loss is, in fact, the loss of our identity. The more we confuse task and role with our personhood and the more satisfaction we draw from role achievement rather than from being persons, the more devastating is the effect of failure on us.

The source of my rage at the reviewer who happened not to like my book was my over-investment in the book. When it was criticized, I felt that I was being attacked and even destroyed.

Ritual

In the midst of the ego trauma associated with losing a coveted award, a significant promotion, or an election to public office, or with having a book manuscript or contract bid rejected or being fired from a job, ritualizing is very difficult. The tournament of life does not arrange consolation games.

The feasibility of any scenario of passage will hence depend on the exact circumstances and on the way each faith community handles its declines in fortune. The following suggestions are not intended as Band-Aids for a very painful experience, but if the situation permits, a scenario such as this may help people accept loss.

Interpretation

Reviewing the facts within the intimacy and confidentiality of a small group may be helpful. When we lose, we often try to ease our pain by finding reasons for that loss in outward circumstances. It is a mature athlete who does not relate his defeat to extraneous causes, even the integrity and competence of the officials. But such feelings are understandable and probably should be ventilated.

A second step may be a review of our personal history, putting our failure or loss into the context of our experience and describing our dreams and ambitions.

It may also be helpful to relate our experience to the insights of biblical faith, perhaps by identifying with certain biblical characters. Not all disappointments have a cause that can be identified. The message of the Book of Job is that our sufferings are not always logical or justly apportioned. Job's deepest pain seems to have been caused not so much by his staggering decline in fortune or even the loss of his family as by the arbitrariness of his disaster. He doubts his own reason and even the reasonableness of the God he has loved and served. At times he feels that he cannot even converse with God in order to hold him accountable. He cries out:

> Oh, that I knew where I might find him, that I might come even to his seat! I would lay my case before him and fill my mouth with arguments. I would learn what he would answer me, and understand what he would say to me. . . . Behold, I go forward, but he is not there; and backward, but I cannot perceive him. On the left hand I seek him, but I cannot behold him; I turn to the right hand, but I cannot see him (Job 23:3-5, 8-9).

Our loss of status from having been betrayed, used, demoted, discounted, and humiliated may seem rationally to have come from our own failures or the actions of others, but the hurt is often so deep and destructive that we cannot avoid laying it on God.

Assimilation

Faced with this situation, how can the small group initiate healing? If in our society identity is so closely related to tasks and roles, what can we do to shift our identity to a less brittle place? Is there a place where we can be made to feel OK about

192

ourselves, where we can ventilate frustrations about ego failures and be given hope that we can go on living effectively?

Myron Madden talks about an ideal retreat center in which there will be a "weeping place." Perhaps the church or the small group can provide for a weeping place or a weeping time for people who recognize the frailties of their humanity, where the career disappointments and frustrations of middle life can be poured out, ritualized, processed, and prayed about.

As a context in which assimilation can go forward, it may be helpful to review the stages in the grief process familiar through the work of Elisabeth Kübler-Ross:

Denial and isolation: Am I tempted to deny the whole business and to run away from it?

Anger: Where am I focusing my anger? Am I sending the mail where it doesn't belong? Do I dare be angry with God?

Bargaining: Am I asking for a reversal of the verdict?

Depression: Can I accept these feelings as understandable or do I need to maintain a facade?

Acceptance: What would acceptance of this event look like and how would that differ from mere passivity?

As another step in the process, it may be well for us to call to mind the distinction between our personhood (identity) and our talents, skills, roles, tasks, successes, defeats, and even our status in the community.[1] What is lost in a disappointment is not unimportant, and the effect on us, if our identity is too closely associated with our role, can be serious. But though much is lost, much remains. Our value as persons remains, as do our gifts of ministry to God and to people.

Intercession

Prayer never seems more real than when it emerges from a place of hurt. The following steps in an intercession addressed to this situation may be helpful:

1. Prayer for the clarification and acceptance of feelings and for greater insight into the situation. As many share prayers as would like.

2. An opportunity for me, as the hurting person, to describe what, if anything, I would like to do about the situation. It is helpful if I am able to walk through some options that occur to me.

3. As part of the clarification, I may want to select one first step in the decision I am considering making.

4. An intercessory prayer by someone in the group for my steadfastness in the decision I will make.

5. Commitment by one or more members of the group to identify with me in my decision and to "hang in" with me through contact, ongoing concern, and prayer.

6. Affirmation of the unity of the group and reassurance that I belong to it and can call on it for love and caring.

194

EIGHTEEN

BIRTHDAYS

Meanwhile, in the midst of other passages, the basic and recurrent passage keeps pace with us. We age and the institutions and arrangements of our lives age with us. Each year we sing "Happy Birthday" and blow out the birthday candles with a little more reluctance and a little more false heartiness. The compensations of age, which sweetened the aging process in simpler times and cultures, are no longer ours. Young people fighting the battles of education and eventual employment look enviously at those who do not have the grace to retire and thus get out of the way.

Small wonder that in America, except for intimate office parties and a clever card, we tend, once we are grown, to ignore birthdays, even the important ones. Europeans are wiser. Not only do they recognize birthdays and "name" days as rites of passage; they give the decennial birthdays special significance. And at one's 50th birthday all the stops are pulled out: flowers, cards, telegrams, festive dinners, speeches, and even pictures and notices

195

in the local newspapers. Later decennial birthdays are also recognized.

Interpretation

Birthdays are good times for sensitive sharing of memories, learnings, and feelings. Unlike the recognition of winning experiences or achievements such as graduation from school, birthdays just happen without our doing much about it except, perhaps, exercising the will to live. This gives us an opportunity to reflect on how much of the substance of the passing year has come to us as a gift. With growing discernment, we realize that even the painful things, which were so hard to assimilate when they happened, may have added to the richness and depth of our existence. (Not that that makes us long for the bad days!) This kind of reflection brings us close to the truth of our own mortality and of the everlastingness of God, as reflected in Psalm 90 and Hebrews 1:10-12.

Some years ago it was my privilege to attend an elegant birthday party in honor of a Swedish friend who had reached 50 years. He was a person of national prominence and the guest list was prestigious. I got to the party by the happy fluke of being an American who had met and befriended our host in the United States.

The party was held in a private dining room of a hotel, and nothing was spared in either food or drink to make it a festive time. After the meal a long time was devoted to toasts, cheers, and speeches in honor of the "birthday child." His achievements, virtues, human qualities were chronicled and extolled, and an atmosphere of warmth and acceptance was created around him. At some point during the evening we all sang with great enthusiasm "O May He Live a Hundred Years." All in all, it was as fine a birthday party as one could wish, and some of its splendor is still with me.

Nevertheless, like most birthday parties, this one had no strategy for dealing with time and its passing. It largely denied it. The next morning at a church service, my friend slipped into a pew not far from us. In the sensitive lines of his face I detected feelings of grief and depression that the party had neither dissipated nor dealt with. I wanted to reach out to him and identify with him in his feelings, but found no way to do it that would have made sense. Nothing in the protocol of birthday celebrations made room for it.

Assimilation

The heart of the birthday celebration is claiming our identity as persons rather than as roles. This brings us in touch with the child within us, which is so much a part of our personhood. On our birthday we are put once more in the center of a circle of love and laughter. We need to claim the feelings that brings.

A simple design for getting back to such feelings is to construct a family album. We fold a piece of regular typing paper into a $5\frac{1}{2}$ x $8\frac{1}{2}''$ folder. On the inside of the folder we draw two ovals on each side. In the ovals on the left side we draw the faces of two people who, when we were small, made us feel secure and allowed us to be a child; on the right side we draw the faces of two people who seemed less patient with us and constantly urged us to be adult. We then share the albums with the group.

This may lead us into sharing some presently joyful child feelings and identifying under what circumstances we experience them. We may also be ready to ventilate some feelings that are painful and embarrassing. We may feel grief about the passage of time and nostalgia for the past; we may be plagued by guilt and regret; we may be anxious about our mortality and fear death.

Paradoxically, a "happy birthday" may be one in which we are not so much encouraged to deny our feelings as to share them with people willing to listen.

Intercession

The King James Version of the Old Testament renders Psalm 90:12, "So teach us to *number* our days, that we may apply our hearts unto wisdom." The New English Bible translates the passage, "Teach us to *order* our days rightly, that we may enter the gate of wisdom."

I am in no position to exegete the Hebrew text, but it is clear that the older translation, in line with the thought of the psalm as a whole, suggests more urgency. To *number* our days, that is, count them and consider how few they are, has a breathlessness that is lacking in "order our days rightly," which sounds like the injunction of a course in efficient office management.

The motif of the intercession in this scenario is "counting our days" so as to recover a sense of how precious they are and to celebrate the temporary. An effective way to do this can be to identify in one-word prayers *one* thing I want to be sure to do with my time while I have it. This need not be grandiose. It may be fishing, tennis, learning French, writing poetry, or doing needlepoint; it may be enjoying my parents, discovering my children, expressing my anger, reflecting, protesting, visiting prisoners, supporting a cause, praying. Whatever it is, sharing it in prayer with the group makes it mine in a special way.

NINETEEN

MOVING

Recent studies on population mobility have raised questions about the truism that moving is a root cause for emotional dislocation in the modern community. It has been assumed that, in the early years of our country, people stayed together and stayed put; hence, they were more able to deal with the shocks of daily life. It is now apparent that throughout our history we have been an exceptionally mobile people.

But whatever the truth about how much we move or how little, moving from one locality to another involves a pain of passage for most people, even for children, who are supposed to handle this better than adults.

When I was nine, my mother, a brother, two sisters, and I left a small village in southern Sweden, where we had lived for about four years, to join my father in America. This was a day we had been hoping and praying for almost two years. In the Swedish village we had for many reasons been considered outsiders: we had a mixed identity (we were both Americans and Swedes) ; we were evangelical Christians and hence suspect; we were not favorites in the blood relationship that was based in the parish; and we had no role in village society. America, on the other hand, was the land of promise. My father had written reports about the life we would experience there and, better yet, had sent Sears & Roebuck catalogs, with a display of toys, horse harnesses, and other luxuries that dazzled us.

But when the day came for us to leave, I did not want to go. My last task was to take a horse tricycle, which had been my friend since I was three, out to a rubbish pile on the edge of the woods. Its wheels were long since gone, but I had dragged it around by the handle bars when I could no longer ride it. I don't remember crying, but when I think about that morning of leavetaking, I still feel grief. That morning everything seemed so dear that I did not want to say good-bye to it: the spruce forests, the little meadows fringed with beech and birch, the friendly stone walls, the checkerboard of tillage around the old gray farm buildings.

For many years, among the industrial squalor of coal and iron cities in America, I mourned the summer land of my childhood. Adults assume that children forget easily, but I have grieved for my village and its surroundings for more than 50 years. When people speak of the trauma of moving, I empathize, for deep inside me a scar remains.

I don't think that the unassimilated grief was all bad, for it led me to an awareness of the meaning of *place* in the shaping of human identity. But I would have gained much by being allowed to work through my grief and to arrive at a balance between the world I inhabited and the one by "hopeless fancy feigned" (Tennyson).

A recent conversation with a friend whose family pattern was a succession of moves from place to place helped me see how important manifest grieving is in transition. The pattern in his family, my friend told me, was to allow no grieving at all. Any available energy was invested in making the new place as alluring as possible. Those in the family who were tempted to cast a longing look over the shoulder were told of the fate of Lot's wife whose tears of regret and nostalgia congealed and turned her into a pillar of salt.

But such strategies probably repress our true feelings, which ultimately take vengeance. A much sounder way to deal with the trauma of moving is to acknowledge its seriousness, ritualize it, and then proceed to interpret and assimilate it.

On our recent visit to Japan, Sally and I met with a group of American missionaries and temporary expatriates. We spent most of a day talking about passages and the value of processing them.

In the group was a former student and dear friend of our family. She was married to an American who had recently been sent to Japan for a tour of duty of several years duration. The assignment came as a surprise both to our friend and her husband. They had been settled in a pleasant community in the eastern part of the United States and had formulated personal plans that the move halfway around the world would seriously disrupt. She was angry about the change and began to wonder, as we often do, where God's will fit into this new pattern for her life.

During the time of preparation for the move and the days of settling into her new community and home in Japan, she felt depressed and resentful. She did not want to believe that leaving dear friends and a fine opportunity for creative ministry in her church could be compensated for by anything in her new situation. She shared some of her angry feelings with the pastor of her new church in Japan, and he suggested that they have a ritual of grief for the past and a celebration of her new life.

She and her husband talked it over and asked the pastor to come to their home. There they shared deep feelings, talked about the good and the bad in the new situation, and committed the present and the future into God's hands. There were tears, prayers, laughter; above all, there was a sense of caring. And although the grief did not vanish, the evening was the starting point of healing and restoration.

The psychological base for a great deal of transitional trauma is the intimate connection between place and identity. Myron Madden says that a woman's home is her body; hence, to change location is like physical crippling for her. I am certain that cultural conditioning is largely responsible for these feelings in women, although Margaret Mead claims that in all human life, as we know it, the woman turns inward toward her home and her children whereas the man turns outward toward his task and associates. But even though this may be true, a man's identity cannot be formed solely by his function. At a deep level he too is at home in place and is affected by transition.

In the spate of immigration literature that has appeared in the last half century, the role of the nostalgic woman who comes to America but never leaves her European homeland is stock in trade. O. E. Rølvaag's appealing character Berit in *Giants in the Earth* comes with her husband and other Norwegian immigrants to the wide prairies of South Dakota, but she shares little of his excitement about the new land. She cruelly misses her home in Norway. She finds the endless oceans of grass confusing and threatening because they provide no resting place for the eye or the spirit. Vilhelm Moberg's Kristina in *The Immigrants* feels similarly disenfranchised by her move from Sweden to Minnesota. She clings to the little mementos she brings with her, reaches out for the rare ministrations of the visiting Swedish Lutheran pastor, and looks back with longing for the poor but cherished life she left behind.

Identity depends on place. My address helps me know who I am. Other things than place also figure in the transitional trauma. There is, for example, the role of relationships. I am helped to know myself by the mirroring provided by intimate friendships. I know who I am to a large extent by looking at the images of me that trusted people give me. This is not to say that I can allow others to impose my self-image on me. We have seen the tragic results of such imposition. Hence, I need to assert my final right to choose the pictures of myself that I find true and acceptable. When I grant this right and responsibility for self-determination, my self-image is unquestionably nourished by the affirmation and caring feedback of the close community of which I am a part.

Physical closeness is necessary for caring to be sustained. Closeness can be provided in part by letter-writing, telephoning, occasional visits, and certainly by prayer. But when I move away, I lose most of my mirrors. Friendship remains, but the system of everyday communications that serves to nourish and shape me as a person is damaged and I feel alone and perhaps isolated. This is the basis for the deep pain that the apostle Paul associates with leaving the people in the churches he has established.

In addition to place and relationship, things such as traditions, history, familiarity, security, and even promise and hope seem fractured when we move away. It may be true, as Myron Madden assures us, that we need to be accepting, for grief "takes a moon to heal." The grief process cannot be hurried, but time alone does not heal these wounds. If the trauma is not dealt with and worked through, our feelings play all sorts of tricks on us, and our grief lives on as resentment or sullenness.

This is the insight of Dante's *Divine Comedy*. The Inferno represents a species of fixation — the bad thing clung to forever. In the Inferno unprocessed feelings, actions, and motives feed on themselves unceasingly. Purgatory represents many of the same things, but here they are subjected to the bitter-sweet medication of grace. The persons on the various terraces of Purgatory are helped to face the reality of themselves without evasion and, with the aid of divine charity, they are enabled to choose those changes in will and behavior that will bring healing.

Paul Tournier's image of the trapeze that must be left behind if the next one is to be seized speaks to the need of letting some things go. The ritual and process that surround moving away should enable us to let go of one trapeze, however safe, and lay hold of another, however risky.

Ritual

This ritual may take place first or last in the process, either when leaving an accustomed place or when arriving at a new one. It should evoke a mood of trust in the presence of the living Christ, that he is with us in all situations, whether familiar or strange. Such a mood can be generated by praying, reading Scriptures (possibly John 14 or Hebrews 11), or singing hymns that have special significance for those making this passage.

A symbolic leave-taking may be represented by the giving and receiving of gifts. The persons leaving entrust certain things to the persons remaining. The persons remaining give the persons moving away a *viaticum* (a provision for the journey) to accompany them.

A moving example of this kind of ritual gift-giving occurs in the story of Mary anointing Jesus in John 12:1-8. The same story is told in Matthew 26:6-13 and in Mark 14:3-9, with some variation in detail. In John's account the anointing takes place at the house of Lazarus, and Mary is the giver of the gift.

The dinner is apparently a testimonial party in Jesus' honor to celebrate the miracle of Lazarus's being raised from the dead. (See W. F. Howard's brilliant commentary in the *Interpreter's Bible*.)[1] Mary has provided a special gift, a pound of expensive perfume, to express her gratitude for a brother restored to life. But the anointing also becomes a gift of leave-taking. And when Judas, out of whatever motives, harshly criticizes her action, Jesus underlines this significance by saying in effect, "She is using some of the nard for this occasion, but she is saving some of it for my burial." In Mark the leave-taking motif is even more clearly stated: "She has done a fine and beautiful thing for me. . . . She did what she could; she poured perfume on my body to prepare it ahead of time for burial" (TEV).

Thus, the nard that was bought to celebrate a resurrection is also used to signify a burial. "Welcome back" and "farewell," coming and going flow together in Jesus' presence. That is the meaning of John 16:16, "In a little while you will not see me any more, and then a little while later you will see me" (TEV). That does not mean that sadness and gladness are the same thing or that resurrection and

207

death cancel out each other. It means, rather, that even in separation and leave-taking, life can be renewed in the presence of the living Lord.

Final elements in this ritual of leave-taking might be an *agape* (love feast) in which bread is shared, or the celebration of a house communion; a benediction; and a hymn. The benediction may be performed by forming a circle or by surrounding the persons involved and by the laying on of hands.

Interpretation

The parting process provides an opportunity for some straight conversation about the problems and promise related to the move. What is gained and what is lost? Was the move decided for the person (as, for example, in military or government service) or was it a choice? How was the move processed in the family? How does the move affect the life and career of the spouse and children as well as other members of the immediate family?

Letting those present who have experienced a traumatic move share the experience can also be valuable.

Such an objective handling of the fact of moving may lead into sharing faith insights derived from the Scriptures. The Bible is largely a book of wandering and pilgrimage. Discussion of the life of Abraham, the exodus, the Babylonian exile, the experience of Jesus, and the missionary journeys of Paul may be helpful.

Assimilation

The final stage of the process is looking honestly at feelings. It may be helpful to share one strong painful feeling and one strong positive feeling associated with the move. If the group is small and personal, everyone can share.

Sometimes the feelings in those who remain behind go beyond grief. They may feel envy, a sense of rejection, hopelessness. Some of this may come out as anger toward those who are leaving. If such feelings are not ventilated, they may live on and have a negative effect on the relationship. Encourage the sharing of such feelings.

TWENTY

RETIRING

Closely related to the experience of losing and the resultant loss of ego esteem is the experience of retiring, or stepping down from positions of responsibility, leadership, and power. Many parents, especially mothers, initially feel they have lost their role when their children leave home. A career disappointment or demotion brings similar feelings, but there is a special pain when society, often arbitrarily, dictates retirement at a certain age. In certain vocational areas this age is now 50 or 55, in others (as in the military and other government departments) it is 60; in most others it is 70.

Attention is now being called not only to the personal trauma that such arbitrariness causes but also to its social wastefulness. People age at different rates; physical energies are usually diminished before mental ones. Hence, in some fields the retirement age is actually creeping up, and formally retired executives, professors, and other specialists are being employed in second careers or as ad hoc consultants.

In Russia recently I saw many older women engaged in street-sweeping and other menial labor. At first glance this seemed heartless. I was used to thinking of older women in retirement homes having their hair set, playing endless games, crocheting, or just sitting. But the women I saw in the streets of Irkutsk may have what the women in the Fairlawn Retirement Home lack—a sense of day-to-day usefulness and of being a part of the active community.

But no matter how we organize our lives or manage to postpone the last day of an active career, we need to accept its inevitability and initiate closure. Such a termination need not mean the end of everything. On the contrary, it can mean a new beginning, especially if I have learned the secret of living with myself.

One reason retirement may be such a traumatic experience is that we may have overidentified much too long with our role, our task, our status, or our power. If I am my job or my power, then the loss of it is death. This is not to say that my job and all that it involves does not enrich me. But if I am only that, I am going to have trouble stepping down.

A friend had been a trusted employee of an organization for many years. He ate, drank, slept, dreamt his work. As the age of 65 approached, he became increasingly edgy and anxious. Finally his panic in being retired became so acute that he committed himself to doing any task whatsoever at no pay in order to stay on board. The same panic has encouraged some businesses to accommodate retiring senior officers by providing them with an office and allowing them to follow the paths they have walked for decades.

But whatever the accommodation, the fact remains: What is over is over. Another sentence is beginning, but we must put a period at the end of this one. As caring people we need to help one another make the decision to let go. Retirement crisis is similar to career crisis, with an important difference. In most crises there is the possibility of a new beginning, but in retiring, we need to face the fact that, no matter how many small new beginnings remain for us, our main career opportunities and our time on the public stage is running out.

Several years ago, when I was inaugurated as a college and seminary president, a colleague of mine from my days at the University of Chicago and a dear friend said to me, with a touch of Jewish melancholy, "Well, Karl, you have reached the top of the ladder. From now on it's all downhill for you."

Retirement is rather like that. There may be pleasant resting places on the way, but the direction is set; we are on our way down. C. S. Lewis, in his last letter, written to Jane Douglass a few weeks before he died, said: "Thanks for your note. Yes, autumn is really the best of the seasons; and I am not sure that old age isn't the best part of life. But, of course, like autumn, it doesn't last." [1]

Ritual

In the professional and business worlds, retirement rituals are a dime a dozen. The ceremonial luncheon or dinner, with a corsage, a plaque, a watch, and maybe a check, and several quasihumorous speeches about the retiree's luxurious future on a Hawaii beach or a Florida golf course, is seen as a necessary interruption of the serious business of business.

I recall a retirement luncheon at which, for some reason, I returned to the meeting room that had been the scene of the festivities a few moments earlier. There was no one left in the room except the guest of honor. He stood clutching his plaque and staring down at the floor as if he had no place to go. His old colleagues and buddies had hurried back to their board rooms and dictating equipment and crowded desk calendars, but he stood surrounded by an emptiness and desolation so intense that I mumbled some inanity and got out of there fast.

Interpretation

How do the churches deal with retirement and closure? Some congregations have ministries to the aging in the form of golden age clubs and senior citizen classes that offer Tuesday afternoon slide showings and bus tours to view the fall foliage.

But something is lacking in the initial grouping. The primary need of aging people is not to be role-determined and lumped as if the role of being old obliterates all other considerations. Old people do, of course, have things in common, things that need to be realistically faced. But old people are also different. They need to be part of society, not apart from it. They need the stimulus of the town or city if that is where they have lived. They need educational and cultural opportunities. They need to be involved in the affairs of the community: meaningful work, creative hobbies, the ongoing activities of churches and clubs. They need generational variety. Above all, they need to feel that they are an appreciated, useful part of family and community.

The scenario of passage should consequently include some sort of group experience in which the meaning of retirement is faced and discussed and its emotional impact assimilated. Discussion topics can be based on Elisabeth Kübler-Ross's steps for handling grief: the temptation to deny reality and the need to deal with it and to accept it.

What is mourned is really the passing of a role identification. The difference between role and personhood should be stressed, along with the possibility of finding new values in growing self-awareness and self-acceptance. (See page 193.)

Although a stage of life is definitely over, all of life has not collapsed because I no longer do what I did. When Tennyson wrote the poem "Ulysses," a dramatic monologue of the Greek hero at the very end of his life, Tennyson was only 33. Two passages are worth quoting: Ulysses is talking to his old companions:

> You and I are old;
> Old age hath yet his honor and his toil;
> Death closes all. But something ere the end,
> Some work of noble note, may yet be done,
> Not unbecoming men that strove with gods.

And a little later:

> Though much is taken, much abides; and though
> We are not now that strength which in old days
> Moved earth and heaven, that which we were,
>   we are;
> One equal temper of heroic hearts,
> Made weak by time and fate, but strong in will
> To strive, to seek, to find, and not to yield.

Tennyson lived to be 83, and it can be argued that the verve he had in 1842 was not his 50 years later. It could also be argued that the mood of Ulysses is not the mood of an old man but that of a young man who, because of circumstance, feels prematurely old.

Nevertheless, we admire old persons like Ulysses who, having discovered and accepted who they are, rejoice in their gifts and the opportunity to use their energies. It seems a relatively rare achievement.

William Faulkner was the great American novelist who was given the Nobel Prize in 1949. I recently read that Faulkner's last years were apparently unproductive and unfulfilling, a gradual falling into ruin. This seems a sad closure for a man as gifted as he was. I intend no judgment, for no one fully understands what age does to us.

Even so imaginative and sprightly a person as J. R. R. Tolkien had a painful old age. After the death of his wife, he returned to some rooms at Merton College in Oxford. His biographer writes:

> In his last years Tolkien felt terribly alone; he
> often complained . . . that he missed his wife
> almost more than he could bear. When he didn't
> work or go out, he often did nothing more than
> sit in his room and stare out of the window,

occasionally whistling or singing to himself. To help alleviate the loneliness he took to visiting other elderly people.[2]

Professor Émile Legouis, in his essay on William Wordsworth, reflects on the English poet's complete swing from youthful liberalism to a petrified conservatism in his later years:

That he was sincere in all his opinions, and that he had strong arguments for his absolute conservatism, cannot be doubted. No apostasy is to be laid to his charge. The evolution of his ideas, which made his old age diametrically opposed to his youth, can be traced step by step, accounted for by outward circumstances and earnest meditations. Yet we cannot help feeling that, all the same, it is a progress from poetry to prose, from bold imaginings to timorousness, from hope to mistrust, from life to death.[3]

In his discussion of old age in *Rhetoric,* for rhetorical purposes Aristotle draws on extreme typology of old age. This typology, which has no exact correspondence to an actual person, nevertheless comes close to the outline of many old people.

They have lived many years; they have often been taken in, and often made mistakes; and life on the whole is a bad business. The result is that they under-do everything. They think but they never know. . . . They are cynical; that is, they tend to put the worst construction on everything. . . . They are small-minded because they have been humbled by life: their desires are set upon nothing more exalted or unusual than what will help to keep them alive. They are not generous, because money is one of the things they must have. . . . They are cowardly and are always anticipating danger. . . . They lack confidence in the future, partly through experience— for most things go wrong, or anyhow turn out

216

worse than one expects; and partly because of their cowardice. They live by memory rather than by hope. . . . This, again, is the cause of their loquacity; They are continually talking of the past, because they enjoy remembering it. . . . Old men may feel pity, as well as young men, but not for the same reason. Young men feel it out of kindness; old men out of weakness, imagining that anything that befalls anyone else might easily happen to them. . . . Hence they are querulous, and not disposed to jesting or laughter—the love of laughter being the very opposite of querulousness (Book 2, Chapter 13).

How can life for those of us who are getting older be better than that? I am sure that biochemistry has something to say about aging and I offer no simple panaceas. I am sure aging people benefit from goal-setting and from discussing principles and values in aging. But I believe the most important resource for older people is a community made up of a variety of people of varying ages, where they can deal with feelings and with the passage of lessening and closure.

Assimilation

I believe group process can be highly effective in dealing with the major emotional problems of age, to the degree that obvious pathology does not stand in the way. It is hoped that these scenarios can be played out in the presence of discerning and caring people of representative ages, but even if that is not possible, much good can come from sharing with one's peers.

The day of or the day after the farewell celebration is a good time to ventilate feelings. This may begin with the retiring person talking to the group about his or her personal history, allowing the person to get in touch with deeper feelings of fulfillment and disappointment around the following questions.

In looking back on my years of service and association, I can identify some gratifying experiences and achievements. The most significant one was

_____, because _____. During those years one of my great disappointments was _____, because _____.

Right now, my most positive feeling is _____. My most painful feeling is _____.

In thinking about the future, I look forward with great expectation to _____. I am anxious about _____.

The second stage of assimilation involves day-to-day adjustment to a new pace and life-style. Sharing feelings continues to be important, although the emphasis will probably shift from the trauma of closure to the pains and pleasures of retirement and retirement activities.

Intercession

Closure and retirement are painful for even the most optimistic. The French have a saying: *Partir, c'est mourir un peu.* It means, "To part is to die a little."

And what we are talking about in lessening and closure is a series of little deaths. Specific concerns and needs should be expressed and prayed about, but in this situation prayer is as much standing together and claiming the presence and grace of the Lord as it is worded petitions.

TWENTY-ONE

FINAL CARING

We need help with the small deaths. And we are going to need a good deal of help with the big one. Despite devastating wars, traffic accidents in the air and on the ground, and news of earthquakes and famines around the globe, we Westerners have managed to push death away from us and to make it unreal. A few decades ago there were many doorways into death. Epidemic diseases, a range of acute body infections, the illnesses of children—all took their toll. So did tuberculosis, diabetes, pernicious anemia, and many undiagnosed ailments. Today even very old people are kept alive by skillful medical maintenance, and life expectancy has increased dramatically.

Even when death is imminent, it is now part of medical strategy to dull its sting by ingeniously compounded and carefully administered medications. People are sedated and anesthetized for death as for major surgery. This removes the anxiety but it may also remove awareness and launder out some of the glory. And part of that glory is our dignity as human beings.

There is hence good sense in what some studies on death and dying are telling us—that human beings should have the opportunity to die with dignity. This means, I presume, not dying like a laboratory animal in drugged oblivion or in snoring anonymity, but facing death, as far as that is possible, with one's eyes open.

I am not sure if that kind of dying is feasible in our highly professional and depersonalized world. We have taken the delivery and the swaddling away from the village women (although there has been some relenting toward fathers being present in delivery rooms since the time I twiddled my thumbs in the O.B. lounge), and we have put the final swaddling into the hands of the night nurse on 3 East, the orderly, and the undertaker.

I have no interest in discrediting professionals. We need them, for they do for us what we have neither the time nor the skill to do. Birth is a scary and messy business, and we have handed it over to the people in the green smocks and the rubber-soled shoes. Death can be even messier and scarier, and most of us are probably relieved that we have to meet it only in the stylized atmosphere of the funeral parlor.

But I have a need for something more, for more involvement, clarity, and support. I would like to be given the grace and the courage to talk about my death with people who honor me by coming on straight.

Interpretation

Years ago, when I was a teacher in a theological seminary, one of our professors developed a malignancy. He continued teaching as long as he had strength. Then one day he went in to see the dean, who had been his colleague and friend for many years. And they talked about his death. The ailing professor had worked out the details of his memorial service, and they talked about that. And then they both cried. In sharing and weeping, they were both comforted.

Assimilation

Such straight conversation leads naturally into something else that weakness and death may bring: the need to be cared for. I am afraid of death, because I need to be in control, and I know death will take my control away. That will be difficult for me, but it may be less difficult if I can entrust myself to the caring community. I would like in my last moments to be swaddled by gentle hands and by them handed over to God's care.

Some images crowd in upon me. I remember the winter of 1944-45. I was evacuated from the front lines around Bastogne and was being transported by army ambulance to a hospital in Luxembourg. When, after a long and tiring ride, we got to the hospital, two towering stretcher bearers picked up my litter from its rack in the ambulance and literally ran up long flights of stairs to the admitting room.

It was an incredible experience. I have never had a sense of being so carefully handled or so well cared for. I felt safe.

A decade ago I saw for the first time Michelangelo's *Pieta* in St. Peter's Basilica. What struck me was not the art, significant as that is, but the sense of helplessness in the form of the dead Christ. I also saw that his being swaddled by his mother recapitulated his swaddling years before in Bethlehem. What I felt in the sculpture was caring, and it aroused in me a deep primal hunger to be thus cared for by those near me in the family of blood and the family of grace when I can no longer care for myself.

I have already quoted some lines from J. S. Bach's song to his young wife, Anna Magdalena. Since the stanza summarizes what I have tried to say, I quote it now in its entirety:

> If thou be near
> Go I with gladness
> To death and to eternal peace.
> Oh, how content were thus my ending,
> If thy dear hands were laid upon me
> And gently closed my faithful eyes.

I believe there is a caring beyond even this caring. But how can we know how right and beautiful that caring is if its truth has not become flesh and touched us through the loving members of the body of Christ?

Caring exercises

One of the most effective ways of getting in touch with the difficulty as well as the beauty of being cared for is the following exercise, which has meant a great deal to me, especially in times of deep discouragement or weariness.

In a small group, select partners. Decide who is to be the carer (A) and who will be cared for (B). B lies flat on the floor, with enough space around for easy movement. A then puts his or her hands firmly under the right leg of B and lifts it very slowly to a comfortable level, then just as slowly lowers it. This act may be repeated. A then proceeds to the left leg, the left arm and the right arm, and finally the head.

This is not a massaging exercise, and neither the limbs nor the head need to be manipulated. A simply lifts the limb or the head of B, who expends no energy whatsoever. B tries to remain "dead weight" to give A a sense of total caring and B a sense of being totally cared for.

Another caring exercise that conveys deep feeling is a symbolic foot washing. It is carried out in pairs. Shoes are removed and each person lightly massages the feet of the other as an act of ministry and caring. It is helpful during this process to share feelings. Is it easy or difficult for me to be cared for in this way? Am I embarrassed about letting another person perform this humble service for me? How does this experience help me understand John 13:1-11?

Epilog

The time for me, my time, is hence not all the "new time." I live and I must die in the "old time," the time of aging and decay. But because, through God's mercy, I also live in the new time, all things have become new. The old time stands on tiptoe waiting for the new.

This is so because I have been buried with Christ in baptism and become a part of his crucified and risen body. Having tasted the waters of baptism, I approach the waters of death and dying with sure hope that death will be no more.

And I do not go alone. Out of whatever need to embrace aloneness, Marcel Proust once wrote,

> The bonds that unite another person to ourself exist only in our mind. Memory as it grows fainter relaxes them, and notwithstanding the illusions by which we would fain be cheated and with which, out of love, friendship, politeness, deference, duty, we cheat other people, *we exist alone.* (Italics mine.) Man is the creature that cannot emerge from himself, that knows his fellows only in himself; when he asserts the contrary, he is lying.

I don't believe that, because I have experienced and experience the contrary every day of my life. What I know about myself I know through the community, supremely through the communion of saints. It is not as if I begin as a solitary creature and seek community. It is because of my communal nature that I can now and then experience myself as solitary. And it is because of my ingrafting in Christ that I occasionally have the clarity to be fully aware of myself as a single, unique person.

Thus companioned, I want to enter the sea and finally make my way to the shore. I know no more realistic or fresher way of saying this than by quoting John 21.

> After this, Jesus appeared once more to his disciples at Lake Tiberias. This is how it happened. Simon Peter, Thomas . . . , Nathanael . . . , the sons of Zebedee, and two other disciples of Jesus were all together. Simon Peter said to the others, "I am going fishing."
>
> "We will come with you," they told him. So they went out in a boat, but all that night they did not catch a thing. As the sun was rising, Jesus stood at the water's edge, but the disciples did not know that it was Jesus. Then he asked them, "Young men [*Paidia*],[1] haven't you caught anything?"
>
> "Not a thing," they answered.
>
> He said to them, "Throw your net out on the right side of the boat, and you will catch some." So they threw the net out and could not pull it back in, because they had caught so many fish.
>
> The disciple whom Jesus loved said to Peter, "It is the Lord!" When Peter heard that it was the Lord, he wrapped his outer garment around him (for he had taken his clothes off) and jumped into the water. The other disciples came to shore in the boat, pulling the net full of fish. They were not very far from land, about a hun-

dred yards away. When they stepped ashore, they saw a charcoal fire there with fish on it and some bread. Then Jesus said to them, "Bring some of the fish you have just caught."

Simon Peter went aboard and dragged the net ashore full of big fish, a hundred and fifty-three in all; even though there were so many, still the net did not tear. Jesus said to them, "Come and eat." None of the disciples dared ask him, "Who are you?" because they knew it was the Lord. So Jesus went over, took the bread, and gave it to them; he did the same with the fish.

This striking scene reminds us of Jesus' first encounter with Peter on the shore of the lake, the episode in the storm in which Peter got into the water to walk to Jesus, and by indirection many other situations in which Peter impulsively led the way.

But the power of the scene for me is also the way it combines the temporal and eternal, the bodily and the spiritual, the personal and corporate character of our passage through time. It hence becomes for me a metaphor of the beginning—as well as the end—of life.

I want my departing to be like that, surrounded by people who exist, not merely as fading memories (Proust), but as members of the body of Christ. Born again and again to a living hope, I want to emerge from the waters of baptism and death and splash my way to the shore.

There will be a fire there, a small glowing center of coals. And there will be bread and fish to eat.

But more than that, there will be people gathered around, all those who love and who await his appearing and his kingdom. And in the midst of the people,

227

like the intensely burning coal at the center of a fire, will be the one whom I have denied and betrayed, misunderstood and borne questionable witness to, failed to trust and certainly to follow, but also loved inexpressibly. He will be in the center. But as I look around, in all the faces that turn toward him, I also see him. His presence is like a flame in them all and on them all. And, miracle of miracle, as I look into the eyes of those nearest me, I know that they are seeing him also in me.

We have all been "under the cloud and in the sea." We have all known and practiced desperate swimming motions to assure our immortality. Now all that is past. We are not here because we were superior swimmers, but because the seas parted. And the life we now face on the other side of death is a life in which beatitude is not merely glimpsed, but known. The apocalypse presents it as a solemn and joyous song of praise around God's throne—a shout of *hosanna* because the battle is over and the victory won. "Worthy is the lamb that was slain."

The final blessing is thus a ritual, a celebration, that points back to all previous rites and is their meaning. Every human ceremony carries with it the pain as well as the joy of passage. The pain is separation from what we know and confrontation with the unknown; the joy is our moving step by step toward fulfillment.

Our final joy is the integrating of all past experience—its brokenness and pain as well as its melancholy sweetness—into God's everlasting today, and the binding together of our fleeting relationships

228

into the peaceable kingdom. And the source of this joy is the lamb who was killed for us and for our salvation. The heavenly song sounds, "You are worthy . . . for you were killed, and by your death you bought men for God, from every tribe, language, nation, and race. You have made them a kingdom of priests to serve our God."

The meaning beyond these splendid images I do not know. Paul tells us that "we will always be with the Lord," and I am content with that. I know that in his presence death and the sting of death have been destroyed, the flailing is over, and we can gladly see and adore that love "which moves the sun and the other stars."

Notes

Chapter 1

1. Daniel Grotta-Kurska, *J. R. R. Tolkien, Architect of Middle Earth* (New York: Warner Books, 1976), p. 153.

2. Quoted by Sven Lidman in *Guds Eviga Nu* (Stockholm: Bonniers, 1936), p. 174.

3. From a column that appeared in the December 19, 1976, Cleveland *Plain Dealer*.

Chapter 2

1. I am indebted to C. S. Lewis for his recovery of the meaning of the word *solemnity*. In popular usage *solemn* has come to mean overly serious, even gloomy. "Solemn as a judge," whatever the original simile meant, now means strict, austere, forbidding. But "solemnizing marriage" means giving it a public, ceremonial character and thus endowing it with the blessing of God and the community. Such stateliness clearly does not rule out joy.

2. The immense and continuing popularity of Gail Sheehy's *Passages*, published in 1976, indicates the universal concern with this topic and the mounting efforts to cope with its personal and social effects.

Chapter 8

1. According to Exodus 13:11-16, the presentation of the firstborn son is rooted in the destruction of all firstborn males among the Egyptians at the time of Israelites' flight from Egypt. The firstborn among the Israelites were spared because of the blood of an animal smeared on the door posts and lintels of their houses. The firstborn were thus ransomed or "bought back" from the Lord by the sacrifice of an appropriate animal. This event is reflected in the rite of presentation, which even in Jesus' day seems to have required an animal sacrifice.

In reporting the presentation, however, Luke draws out none of the sacrificial implications. He does report that Jesus' parents offered a sacrifice of a pair of doves, but this may have been in connection with Mary's purification. In that rite poor people were permitted to substitute two pigeons for the prescribed lamb.

The bloodier aspects of the presentation, that is, the sacrificial theology, may be suggested in the cryptic words of Simeon: "This child is chosen by God for the destruction and the salvation of many in Israel. He will be a sign from God which many people will speak against and so reveal their secret thoughts. And sorrow, like a sharp sword, will break your own heart" (Luke 2:34-35 TEV).

The passage seems to have some "Egyptian" echoes. Just as the presence of Israel in Egypt was a source of both destruction and salvation, so the presence of the Messiah in Israel will have ambivalent effects. But the price of the presence is the blood of the firstborn. Hence the sorrow like a sharp sword.

In the context of this book, the identification of Jesus with all firstborn males is not unimportant. In that respect too he was with us.

2. This age is based on the chronology of Matthew and Luke 3:23, but John, whose grasp of time and place is often accurate, quotes some of the Jewish leaders as saying to Jesus, "You are not even fifty years old—and you have seen Abraham?" (John 8:57 TEV). Why fifty, if that was not roughly accurate, since a lower age would have given strength to their arguments? But here, as in other matters relating to the historical person of Jesus, we are left unsure.

3. The word *greater* is used several times in New Testament writings to indicate the contrast between Jesus and his predecessors (Matt. 12:41; Heb. 1:4, 9; 3:3).

4. In the apostolic preaching recorded in Acts as well as in other passages in Acts (1:22, 10:37, 11:16, 13:24-25, 19:3-4), the gospels' portrayal of John's role is consistently supported.

5. The marked difference between the first three gospels and that of John was recognized very early. Origen calls John's gospel a "spiritual" gospel. This does not mean that John's gospel is not to be seen as history. It means that, more than the other evangelists, the writer of John's gospel saw the data from the point of view of the resurrection and the exaltation of our Lord.

6. The dramatic difference between the Gethsemane struggle of our Lord as recorded in the first three gospels and in John is suggested by Jesus' word to Peter, as given in John's gospel, after the latter has cut off the ear of Malchus. John's account tells us that Jesus says to Peter, "Put your sword back in its place! Do you think that I will not drink the cup of suffering which my Father has given me?" (John 18:11 TEV).

The word is spoken in the Garden not far from the spot where, according to the synoptics, Jesus in terrible agony had asked that precisely that "cup" be allowed to pass. It may be argued that John is recording the acceptance and equanimity that *follow* the struggle of Jesus, but this argument would be more convincing if John had allowed us to catch a glimpse of that struggle.

It is hard to escape the conclusion that John's messianic scenario for Jesus is different from that of the synoptics. This does not make it invalid, but it makes it different. Even the poignant reflection of Jesus on his suffering in John 12:22-28 (which may be a Gethsemane echo) has a clear counterpoint of "glory." Jesus concludes his statement by saying, "Now is my heart troubled—and what shall I say? Shall I say, 'Father, do not let this hour come upon me'? But that is why I came—so that I might go through this hour of suffering. Father, bring glory to your name!" (TEV). Nothing quite like this softens the starkness of the Passion account in the synoptics.

7. Matthew and Mark refer to the incident but omit much of Luke's detail.

8. Jeremiah (7:11) speaks of the temple being made into a "den of robbers." Isaiah (56:7) refers to it as "a house of prayer." Malachi (3:1) prophesies that the Lord "will suddenly come to his temple."

Chapter 9

1. In *Jesus Christ, Superstar* the Gethsemane prayer has a true pre-Easter desperateness, striking a most authentic note.

2. The gospel of John presents special problems in relation to the twelve. The full list is never named. Chapter 21 speaks of seven disciples, but only three are mentioned by name: Simon Peter, Thomas, and Nathanael (who, incidentally, is not mentioned by the synoptics). Two of the remaining four are the sons of Zebedee (presumably James and John, although they are not mentioned by name). The other two are spoken of as disciples, but we don't know who they are.

The "beloved disciple" has traditionally been thought to be John, one of the two sons of Zebedee, but some scholars dispute this. If we assume that the beloved disciple was not John, the group at the lakeside included Peter, Thomas, Nathanael, James, John, the beloved disciple, and one other. Since John's gospel mentions only ten disciples specifically, we must conclude that the seventh one present at Tiberias was Andrew, Philip, or the other Judas. The seventh may well have been Andrew, since he is most often grouped with Peter, but we don't know.

The disciples figure much less prominently in John's gospel than in the synoptics. In conformity with John's apparent purpose, the function of the disciples in John's gospel seems to be to *see* the revelation of glory rather than to be instructed and empowered for mission (see John 1:35-

51). That they did not always *see* Jesus is evident from his efforts, especially in the final discourses, to explain himself to them (John 13–17).

3. Mark gives a short list of these women and adds, "Many other women who had come to Jerusalem with him were there also" (Mark 15:41 TEV).

Chapter 15

1. See 1 Corinthians 7:8 and 9:5.

Chapter 17

1. See the discussion of the Twin Towers in my book *Meet Me on the Patio* (Minneapolis: Augsburg, 1977), pp. 39-68.

Chapter 19

1. W. F. Howard, "The Exegesis of John," *The Interpreter's Bible* (Nashville: Abingdon, 1952), Vol. 8, p. 655.

Chapter 20

1. W. H. Lewis, ed., *Letters of C. S. Lewis* (New York: Harcourt, Brace & World, 1966), p. 308.

2. Grotta-Kurska, *J. R. R. Tolkien*, p. 222.

3. *The Cambridge History of English Literature* (New York: MacMillan, 1933), 11, pp. 120-21.

Epilog

1. *Paidia* in Greek usually means "children," even infants of both sexes, but it may be used "as a form of familiar address on the part of a respected person who feels himself on terms of fatherly intimacy with those whom he addresses" (W. Bauer, *A Greek-English Lexicon of the New Testament*). So here. The RSV "children" seems much less effective in this context.